1000 IDEAS BY 100 GRAPHIC DESIGNERS

1000 IDEAS BY 100 GRAPHIC DESIGNERS

MATTEO COSSU

BEVERLY MASSACHUSETTS

ROCKPORT PUBLISHERS

Copyright © 2009 by **maomao** publications
First published in 2009 in the United States of America by
Rockport Publishers, a member of
Quayside Publishing Group
100 Cummings Center
Suite 406-L
Beverly, MA 01915-6101
Telephone: (978) 282-9590
Fax: (978) 283-2742
www.rockpub.com

ISBN-13: 978-1-59253-574-3
ISBN-10: 1-59253-574-7

10 9 8 7 6 5 4 3 2 1

Publisher: Paco Asensio
Editorial coordination: Anja Llorella Oriol
Text edition: Matteo Cossu
Art director: Emma Termes Parera
Layout: Maira Purman
Introduction translation: Cillero & de Motta Traducción

Editorial project:
maomao publications
Via Laietana, 32, 4th fl, of. 104
08003 Barcelona, Spain
Tel.: +34 93 268 80 88
Fax: +34 93 317 42 08
www.maomaopublications.com

Printed in China

Contents

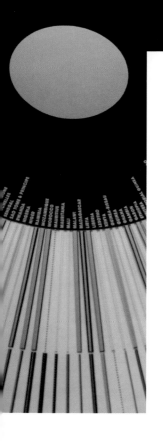

NEPOMUK

DESIGN

ILLUSTRATION

SHOP

CONTACT

LINKS

1,000 Tips, 1,000 Pictures and a Game of Connect Four

Matteo Cossu

We conceived this book with the idea of a textbook in mind. Nevertheless, when trying our hand at the challenge of giving it a didactic slant, we were faced with a harsh reality. Do you remember high school? Or better yet, junior high? Long hours of staring blankly at a book alternated with chewing pencil tops and reading the same sentence over and over again. The texts seemed endless even when they were only short lectures—and it seemed they were trying to ransack our teenage angst-ridden thoughts. In an attempt to deconstruct the essence of a textbook, we traveled back to those pimply years rationalizing what it was that drove us away. Grief, despair, and a recess of that angst still emerged but the answer was clear: those books imposed their knowledge on us. If we wanted to teach without wearing the uncomfortable shoes of a teacher, if we wanted to address important and interesting issues in contemporary graphic design without being cocky, presumptuous, or uselessly scholarly, then we were called on to find a new concept. A book that would be, yes, didactic but at the same time direct, non-exclusive, and that transmitted knowledge from peer to peer. As we tied all the elements together it became clear that it was like a puzzle, or a game of wit. A lot like Connect Four. We'd hereby like to describe the whole book-making process while…playing the game against ourselves.

We began from disc one—analyzing our bookshelves and the design bookshops noting that it would be very interesting to put out a new kind of publication on the subject; something that had communicative strength and possessed a desire to share and a will to expose the day-to-day, step-by-step reverberation of design. The title inscribed itself perfectly in our perception. It's a fact that the old Sanskrit root of the word "thousand" points to tavas, the suffix for "strong." This concept of strength is exactly what we appealed to in order to push through the foundation idea for this publication.

This book aims to be more about designing than design. We intended to reveal the daily practice of the craft more than just the exhibition of the crafted. Hence, our concept traveled on these model tracks, and slowly took form. We needed a format that could condense as much information as possible; something that would be easy to read, quick, and attention-capturing.

So the idea of the "tip" was born—a small but useful piece of practical advice, encompassing the widest gamut of formats and expressive forms and explaining the most varied aspects of the trade. We explained to contributor designers that they should envision the tips as if in the context of an instruction manual; in a perfect framework of cross references and links, like a cut-through image of their own creative essence, or of their more global approach to design. We briefed designers on this general intent, but we steered especially clear of imposing any restriction in length or style of writing. We are strong believers in graphic design as a desire, a dreamy thought of expression, with its applied facets of course, but with the ultimate goal of entertainment, reinterpretation, and visual proposals—new visions of old ideas. In one word, creativity. And just like that, it was time to move to disc two on our metaphorical connect four board.

The texts from the designers yielded bewildering results. We couldn't have asked more of the designers and they have been terribly responsible in this respect, following the brief to perfection, each one interpreting and customizing it to the fullest of their talent. The finished tips represent all the tones in a range that goes from conceptual one-word keywords, to wisdom—enriched quotes, up to mini-essays.

Ze Paz's (www.zedapaz.com) very personal reinterpretation's of the classic Connect Four game.

Inside the 1,000 the designers made space for themes such as inspiration seeking, designer's block, the genesis of the idea, the conditions most likely to generate an idea, the difficulties of production, the different influences, the ethics involved in designing and communicating, the most appreciated textbooks, and the creatives each of us look up to. But this is no strictly theoretical book. There are also a lot of less glamorous aspects, such as the production side of design and the countless times we curse our printers, software, deadlines, bosses, clients, interns, or the weather. Another important part of the tips was dedicated to sharing actual details such as finishes, color combinations, fonts, add-ons and plug-ins, and special software. This is particularly meaningful, because it means that many designers still have their feet on the ground. It means that many of them still see the design process as a sort of housebuilding in which the mason-designer needs not only an instruction manual and a project, but also solid, direct advice, shared and given unconditionally.

As you will see just by flipping through the pages, this book also has a very strong graphical identity, rich and heterogeneous—someone might even argue against a certain lack of uniformity. Nevertheless, this graphical connotation is an editorial choice and a direct consequence of the brief. Designers were asked to supply ten images to go along with the ten tips. As for the texts, we wanted the images to assume a somewhat didactic incline in the quality and theme of the images supplied. In conclusion there was complete freedom regarding theme, technique, and format. It's been a point of dispute whether under this rule the publication would lose order and certain rigidity necessary for ease of comprehension. We believe to have made the right choice. We were again amazed by the richness of the material that started to happily fill our mailboxes, both virtual and real. The material supplied to us is even more diverse and distinct than the texts themselves. Many designers decided to advise the reader about the numerous abstract aspects of designing. Some decided to investigate the pros and cons of order versus chaos finding, as Plato did, the overlapping limbs of both (see the Timaeus); others instructed on the attitudes to keep while dealing with clients, providers, or the clerk that won't give back correct change.

Featured in the book you'll see illustrations—beautiful hand-drawn sketches, lo-fi post-it art, ironic vectorials, iconic vectorials, and austere typographic visuals. Custom-made illustrations had the advantage of being more direct, but banality never even surfaced in any of the projects. Other designers decided to accompany their tips with photography—beautiful and meticulous, like in the case of Tom Cramshaw's black—and—white renderings of tropical plants, or the no-less gracious hand-picked impromptu pictures of Heesun Seo reminding the good old times of Polaroids more than the glacial unfriendliness of this digital era. Her subjects are in motion representing stillness, or still, representing motion. Lighting is bright and cheerful or unlit and contrasting. On another plane, Jessica Scheurer used darkness that tinged everyday objects to illustrate her ideas. In between, rests a full kaleidoscope of photographical expression and assorted mixing of techniques.

All these images have one common denominator, and it would be erroneous to think that designers took this task lightly, providing just any old picture. The 1,000 pictures share a collective origin—spontaneously or through more complicated processes they were conceived to express or accompany the content in the text.

This observation lead us to move disc three. We asked ourselves how to interpret all these connections that designers made. Between their intent of communicating and sharing wisdom, between their choice of words and writing style and the picture they selected to illustrate the two above. Believing that such a mountain of data could definitely be mined, numbers plotted and conclusions drawn, we realized the need for a smooth ramp to take the reader on this printed journey. We thought that this could be achieved by accompanying this more practical prologue with a bird's eye theoretical view on design. We decided to put it all in the very capable hands of Luz del Carmen Vilchis Esquivel, PhD. Through the outlook of her experience in the academic side of graphic design, she dissected and elevated all the design jargon into a lucid recollection of what it is to be a designer, what it means to understand design and, most importantly, how visual messages are coupled with written word with the intent to pass on knowledge.

When we had to make the selection for the 100 designers, we based ourselves on the fact that any level of experience has precious viewpoints that are interesting to share. Included are designers of all levels. Some of them are pioneers in their fields, most of them have seen their work endorsed and prized in international awards, the great majority of them is regularly featured in graphic design blogs and specialized magazines. But there was no formal filter of age or "experience" in the selection. The 100 designers or studios that take part in this book range from industry gurus, to independent artists cross-pollinating into design, to fresh out of school students with exceptional perspectives and views on design.

We are strong believers of the horizontal aspect of graphic design. And although—as in any discipline—there is a now, and there is a then, hierarchies are made to be subverted, and we believe that any creative person, no matter the experience or the preferred field of expertise can enlighten or guide the reader. Because our life experiences are all inevitably one of a kind. Our creativity becomes comprehension through life experiences. And magically, as coming out of a brainstorming tunnel there we were, the final move of our strategy, the diagonal section connected with disc four. And the game was closed.

Knowledge is strength, and freedom is strength. But freedom can only come from the transmission of what we know, from teaching and from passing on the skills that we got from others. Freedom comes from being part of this cycle that takes any discipline, not only graphic design, to continually shape itself into new forms, melt and dry to melt again in an endless Heraclitean continuum of reinventions.

All in all, we want these 320 pages to rest undusty on your shelves, we'd like to be included in your daily routines, to be there with the cereal and with the deadline-driven-late-night-slumber-eyed-coffee-tasting last mouse clicks before handing in, smartly dressed but with mismatched socks. We want you to carry the book in your oversize bag, we want you to use it as your grandmother's cookbook when cooking for your sweetheart, or better we want you to keep it through the years and maybe use it as a gift for the next generation of graphic designers this world will see.

While orchestrating the next move in our "game," we decided to analyze the 1,000 tips for recurring keywords, and guess what? Keeping in mind that the bigger the word, the more recurrent it is in the text, it seems that playing and having fun are two fundamental messages that our 100 designers wanted to communicate.

Understanding Design from a Design Perspective

Luz del Carmen A. Vilchis Esquivel, PhD

1,000 Ideas by 100 Graphic Designers is a cumulus of ideas that do not generally crop up in the everyday world of graphic design. As a matter of fact, one would be hard pressed to actually hear a graphic designer's voice. We know designers through their designs, as professionals immersed in a project, whether traditionally pouring over a desk and drawing sketch after sketch in an indefatigable factory of ideas, or in a digital space, generating alternatives from a core concept.

The ideas in the design are always for the design; designers think about the message, they interpret it, and give it a meaning that encompasses the central significance as well as underlying ones; they choose the ideal medium or mediums for the conception and carry out a series of functional steps to achieve a final result: the design creation.

Nevertheless, talking about this process is not easy. It requires a great introspective effort, "directing attention towards the design itself," towards the designer's personal trajectory, towards a series of lessons from experiences that have left a permanent imprint on the individual. It also requires an attitude of generosity to distill all this information, and extract fragments of knowledge and know-how.

In the Shoes of a Graphic Designer

When we imagine 1,000 ideas on graphic design, we can compare this concept with the well-known basic guide of colors that unfolds like an attractive range of tones, saturations, and levels of shininess, which can be combined to create the 16 million colors available to us on the digital color pallet.

The first pillar of these tips is an accumulation of years of practice and knowledge on composition, on a structure's values, on visual literacy, about semantic characteristics, degrees of iconicity, frameworks, or, in a nutshell, a mastery of visual grammar.

There are also aspects relating to genre, that is, decisions about the best means to transmit the message through the right medium, in relation to the assortment of objects encompassed in design: books, magazines, newspapers, annual reports, packaging, promotional materials, posters, wall advertisements, mobile publicity, architectural signage, corporate identities, to complex visual structures such as campaigns, signage systems, corporate identities, brands and products, without forgetting the full scope of linear and nonlinear narratives, ranging from comic strips to animation and multimedia graphics.

Finally, there are the determining factors of all visual communications, the different purposes for which the design is made, taking into account the special ways of communicating with issuers and receivers: publicity, propaganda, educational or cultural material, informative design, indicative design, even ornamental or plastic design.[1]

Each of these modalities refers to specific values of the message and important rhetorical resources. Graphic designers have to constantly oscillate between the visual rhetoric for seducing, persuading, or convincing, and the rhetoric of implication and exaltation, or between the rhetoric of learning and the information being transmitted to the borders of aesthetics and leisure.

[1] Vilchis Esquivel, *Diseño. Universo de conocimiento*, p. 11-28.

The Imprints of Design

Our understanding graphic design expresses our most immediate thoughts: knowledge arising from the perception of the design object upon capturing its characteristics, contrasts in shape and color and the quality of the means, the efficiency of the medium, and its external relations. Understanding is explaining, unfolding the design, detailing its contents and understanding its significance. As Jorge Frascara explains, "The design of visual communication is an intellectual, social, aesthetic, and practical discipline, which consequently involves many levels of human abilities: power of analysis, mental flexibility, clarity of judgment, visual refinement, technical knowledge, manual skills, cultural awareness and ethical responsibility."[1]

Understanding graphic design is also going deep into the object being designed, transferring its forms and grasping it, squeezing it, hugging it, making it something intimate and personal, making it part of you, melting it, sharing it. It is a profound act of interpretation that explains and justifies the motives of the graphic design.

Recapitulating, the designer redirects his attention towards his own design and judges the essential elements to be able to express them in words, describing and committing the word that expresses the fundaments of that which is known.

The knowledge of what has been designed here takes on importance in the voices of those who accept the risk of increasing their commitment to the design in a collective action, in the need to identify their thinking in specific ideas, more specifically, constructing an ideology and directing attention toward the design's social impact.

This journey goes beyond bringing the design to life. It does not peter out in the explanation, rather it focuses on human effort and involves conscious ethical, sociological, anthropological, and aesthetic considerations, integrated in a conceptual compilation that, on different levels of graphic design, constitutes what is called global vision, objective spirit, or ideology.

Participating in an act of reflecting on, evaluating and disseminating the graphic design, from a practical and personal perspective, is an external manifestation, an act of definition stemming from the discovery of the self, and it involves deliberation, intention, and purpose. "It is important to grasp the design with liberty…our lives and thoughts actually have a comprehensive nature…we should have the liberty to examine the design…through this process of interaction, new impulses are obtained in the creation of new designs…"[2]

Listening to the Voices of Designers

Graphic design, impregnated with its origins of a deep practical meaning, cannot evade the many ideas and approaches generated by human behavior.

For this, it is important to understand graphic design, in each of its facets and as a whole, in each stage of the process and as a finished project, as this implicitly contains the interpretation of the discipline itself which, just like any other area of human knowledge, requires maximum effort in the generation of ideas.[3]

Understanding design in this way is the task of intelligence, which identifies the needs and sets out the alternative solutions. The variety of interpretative conceptions affirms, in all the tones and for the different reasons, the diver-

Luz del Carmen A. Vilchis Esquivel, PhD

Mexican. Postgraduate Professor of the National School of Visual Arts (ENAP) of the National Autonomous University of Mexico (UNAM). She is a member of SIN-CONACYT and the Design Research Society. She studied Graphic Design and Philosophy and also has a Master's degree in Communication and a PhD in Fine Arts from Spain and in Philosophy from Mexico. She has published nine books on graphic design and sixty-one articles, collaborated in eleven works and reviewed forty-three international articles. She assists in preparing programs in various universities, teaching and delivering numerous national and international conferences. She has carried out professional graphic design projects for companies in several countries, and has exhibited her works in more than forty sole and group exhibitions in Mexico and abroad. She has management experience in private initiatives and was Director of the ENAP of the UNAM.

[1] Jorge Frascara, *El diseño de comunicación*, p. 165. [2] Takenobu Igarashi, «Mi relación con el diseño», p. 37.
[3] Dr. Luz del Carmen A. Vilchis Esquivel, *Diseño. Universo de conocimiento*, p. 11-28.

sity of the arguments and the multiplicity of the currents that coexist in design spheres, and which give shape to interests and aspirations in daily life, in graphic language, and in society's visual culture.

As Tomás Maldonado said in a visionary way, communication that does not fulfill the demands of "living dialog between men of the same era" does not comprehend its meaning. Communication, stated the author, is not a resource of solitary persons but of social individuals in everyday situations.[1]

The most important of all this is that despite the plurality of trends, methodologies and projects that are expressed about and from design, the deeper aspects of their comprehension are a common denominator underpinning the theory and practice of the discipline.

This is a space of professional perspectives, an interesting collaboration between counterparts that will cause the conception of the design and the design creation to differ. This didactic sequence, formed of tips that transform the design of today into a series of flexible and changing fields of knowledge, are points of reference to resolve and identify designs' needs and solutions.

Trajectories of the Perspective, Itineraries of Ideas

This variety of responses and explanations opens a horizon enabling the dominant aspect of graphic design to shed its "we do" aspect, to open the way for "we plan" against which the design reaffirms its creative capacity, from this diversity of clear, intelligible, and hence, didactic stances, that enable the design to be always seen as an innovative unit.

All the ideas shown demonstrate the variability of methods, and show the plurality and complexity of projects, leading graphic design through routes that have the parallel capacity to guide amateurs, students, and professionals.

Here the designer is not presented as a monolithic being, an inflexible element, or glorified figure;[2] instead, emphasis is placed on the fact that graphic design is as much a practice as a concept and that its cultural context, added to the designer's profile, is a sphere that converges with other spheres to create a single universe of knowledge.

True communication in graphic design therefore entails knowing the special meaning of imaginary visual aspects with emphasis on the importance of meaning, legibility, and the potential to interpret any kind of visual text.

After understanding design as a process, an intervention, and a group of actions, it is feasible to read the characteristics in each of its parts as evidence of the analysis of its visual grammar, its framework, its genres and discourses, or in its expression as a whole, that is, as a synthesis of a representative and singular medium. In any of these options, thought and speculation on the design creation always generate maturity and an awakening in the designer himself.

Graphic design thus shows the need for a constant interpretation and analysis of its variants from stances that do not compromise or pleasure themselves, but on the contrary, demonstrate the rigor with which a designer is able to qualify himself and evaluate his work.

Each conjecture presented here is in itself a moment of reflection on the "thinking" and

---

[1] Tomás Maldonado, *Escritos preulmianos*, p. 91-93. [2] Penny Sparke, *An Introduction to Design and Culture*, p. 1-9.

"doing" of the design, which opens the way to pursuing responsibility in its application in the education and professionalization of future graphic designers. This is the perfect fusion of theory and practice.[1]

This work seeks evidence of the budgets that make the design possible and its insertion into visual culture in concise capsules that show: the dimension of the designer, the replicas of countless questions about the design creation, the identification of the alternatives given as a set of visual correlations and notes to identify each of his projects, the structure of meaning and its translation into written gestures as responses to stimuli that favor each decision in the design process.

We must show appreciation for these thoughts in the form of tips or short ideas, whose operations of recognition and internalization of contexts and experiences explore the strategies of graphic design and its vestiges in thought: "The essential relationship of the imagination with reason and the consequent conversion of the entire anthropological route in a semantic journey,"[2] that is, the meaning in the imprints of the design creation.

When the behaviors of the designers and their conditions for creativity are identified, when the conditions of application of their own skills and qualities are determined, when the personality of the designer is established in a completed and resolved design, only then can the graphic design be truly understood.

Conclusions

The graphic designer, issuer and receiver of his own messages and those of other people, is responsible for what he does; and upon manifesting himself in his designs, he responds with his work to communicative intentions and their integration with the purposes of others' common purposes.

The express responsibility of the designer on visual messages issued in a public medium is the duty of intelligence and imagination. The codes of the design and their configuration in the design creation are catalogs of behavior that the responsibility of designing generates according to the communication needs of each culture.

The role of graphic design is a commitment to the form and its imperatives, one way of creating an obligation with the design creation, including direction, competence, demand, antagonism or concurrence—specific details based on the routine nature of everyday life and the existence of principles that ultimately form the foundations supporting the discipline.

Each of the designer's requirements is manifested as a skill—a natural ability that enables him to realize a creative behavior—but this generic attitude is formed and learned across time, the designer acquires knowledge, methods, technical skills and is particularized to constitute the dominion of what really matters here: graphic design.

Bibliography

Babolín, Sante. *Producción de sentido*. Bogotá: Universidad Pedagógica Nacional, 2005.

Coumans, Anke. "The visual essay. Reflexivity in the design process". *The Reflexive Zone*. Utrecht: Utrecht School of the Arts, 2004.

Frascara, Jorge. *El diseño de comunicación*. Buenos Aires: Infinito, 2006.

Igarashi, Takenobu. "Mi relación con el diseño". *Ensayos sobre el diseño*. Buenos Aires: Infinito, 2001.

Maldonado, Tomás. *Escritos preulmianos*. Buenos Aires: Infinito, 1997.

Ricard, André. *Diseño. ¿Por qué?* Barcelona: Gustavo Gili, 1982.

Sparke, Penny. *An Introduction to Design and Culture*. London: Routledge, 2005.

Vilchis Esquivel, Luz del Carmen. *Diseño. Universo de conocimiento*. Mexico: Claves Latinoamericanas, 1999.

---

[1] Anke Coumans, «The visual essay. Reflexivity in the design process», p. 19-27. [2] Sante Babolín, *Producción de sentido*, p. 49.

1000 Tips

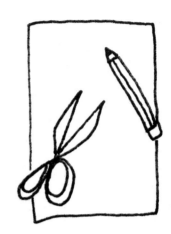

1 TRUST YOUR INSTINCTS. Your first thought is usually the right one or at least the correct place to start from.

2 KEEP IT REAL (OR NOT). I once heard Michael Wolf (of Wolf Olins fame) describe the design process as like traveling through a house full of different kinds of rooms. I remember him saying "don't get caught in the inspiration room for too long." I always liked this thought. I guess it's a bit like watching too much reality TV, you begin to think its real life.

3 ALWAYS ALLOW TIME TO PLAY. You can think of ideas till your heart's content but unless you allow the time to play it will only ever stay in your head.

4 SURROUND YOURSELF WITH TALENTED INDIVIDUALS. It is an old adage but very true; you are only as good as those you work with.

5 THE DESIGN OUTCOME IS IMPORTANT BUT THE PROCESS IS PARAMOUNT. If you can't enjoy the "working" and become too focused on the "result" it will always end in disappointment— 95% of the time if you enjoy your process the result will be great anyway.

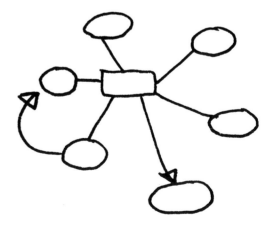

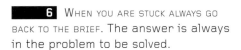

6 WHEN YOU ARE STUCK ALWAYS GO BACK TO THE BRIEF. The answer is always in the problem to be solved.

7 Work in an environment that inspires you.

8 SURROUND YOURSELF WITH PLANTS. Give them a name. Water them. It's surprising how the simplest of activities can generate a positive outlook on your work.

9 INVEST IN A GOOD DESK CHAIR. It's a whole lot better outlaying a lump of cash for a great chair than seeing it disappear two-fold at your physiotherapist.

10 Play lots and lots and lots and lots and lots of ping-pong.

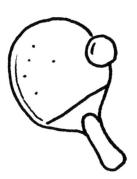

21-19
www.21-19.com

Good design begins with asking questions, initiating a dialogue that informs the creative outcome and results in beautiful, purposeful design. 21-19 are proponents of dialogue: between themselves and the clients, within their creative team and with their suppliers, and ultimately, through the designs they create and the audiences they engage. The executions of their designs are limitless, the breadth of the creative approach leads them to consider possibilities beyond the brief—an approach that has been paramount to success. They claim to have been fortunate to work with people who understand the potential of good design and seek sophisticated and compelling design solutions; however they are not afraid to work with clients new to design, taking them on an exploration, a direction they may not have previously considered.

Alan van Roemburg

www.alanvanroemburg.com

Born in Melbourne, Alan van Roemburg spent most of his adolescence in the Netherlands before returning to Australia at 16 to begin his studies in design. He graduated from Swinburne University National School of Design in 2005 with a Bachelor of Multimedia Design and was awarded a scholarship for honors. Alan has worked for numerous prestigious design agencies, among them David Trewern Design. Clients include Arologic, Certified Practicing Accountant Australia, Parkslide Enterprises, and Paul Barbera Exhibitions.

Now 26, he owns and operates his own design firm in Melbourne. Alan's desire to continually evolve as a designer has led him to explore many different design disciplines, from from web and logo design, to print and packaging.

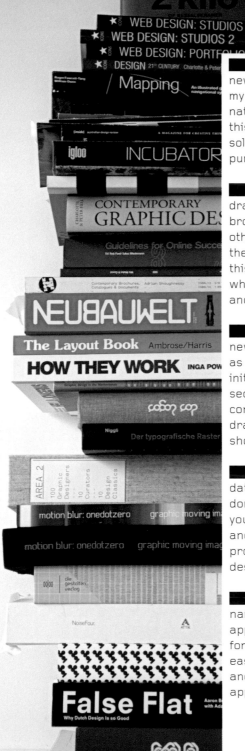

11 RESEARCH. When engaging in a new project, regardless of the discipline, my first step is research. Understand the nature, audience, and subject matter as this enables you to find the appropriate solution therefore bringing meaning and purpose to the design.

12 COLLECT. I have boxes and drawers full of magazines, flyers, brochures, books, leaflets, and many other odds and ends I have collected over the years. Organize your materials, as this can often be the best place to start when drawing for new inspiration. Collect and collate materials.

13 CONCEPTUALIZE. When beginning new projects, brainstorm as many ideas as possible in no particular order. Avoid initial critiquing, over-thinking, and second-guessing as this breaks the conceptual process. The key is to keep drawing and evaluate later. Multiple short sessions work best.

14 SKETCHES AND RECORDS. Order, date, and maintain your sketches and don't forget to keep copies. This allows you to develop, build or stimulate ideas and is also a record of the process to prove intellectual property over your designs.

15 STRUCTURE. Setup the structure, namely grids and typography. Correct application of these elements allows for consistency in design. It is also the easiest way to organize information and different elements while remaining appealing and harmonized to the viewer.

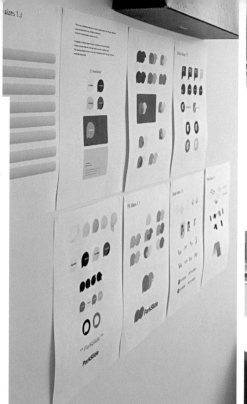

Mandarin Orie
Tokyo, Japan

16 PRACTICE AND STUDY. Like many designers I started my career being overly creative without much thought for structure. As I gained more experience, I began to realize that more often than not, simplicity and structure is the correct method. Practice design and study it.

17 CLIENTS. Be well prepared for meetings with clients and research beforehand. This will not only impress them, but will also allow for a more effective meeting. Clients will appreciate time spent with them. Time is money, so use it wisely.

18 HAVE FUN. Often the best results come when the mind is free and relaxed. If you hit a mental block, take a break and find a distraction to free your mind then re-examine the problem later. My other passion is music so I like to have a mix on the turntables to regain inspiration.

19 WORKSPACE. Keep a well-organized and tidy workspace. Avoid clutter and make sure you have plenty of inspirational material that is readily accessible. Surround yourself with material and inspiration that relates to the current project you're working on.

20 DIVERSIFY. Running a multi-disciplinary design studio can be hard, but rewarding. Exploring different design disciplines involves learning and research must follow very similar rules and practices. The understanding of a wide range of disciplines can assist in design success and can further business opportunities.

Ternstroemiaceae.

Camellia The...

21 HAVE TEA WITH YOUR CLIENT. It is important to sit down with the client and spend time discussing the project. That way you become confident about the brief and what is required of your role as designer.

22 ALLOW PLENTY OF TIME FOR THE IDEA TO COME TOGETHER. Mull the job over in your mind before starting to produce visuals. Think about it while you're on your way to work, sitting on the bus, cooking dinner, at the cinema, etc.

23 AVOID GOING TO DESIGN BOOKSHOPS FOR INSPIRATION. The seductive visuals distract you from the client's brief, and therefore the content of what you are designing.

24 TIDY UP. For me it is important to tidy my desk before I start on a new project. This way my attentions are focused on the project and are not distracted by mess lurking underneath. I have to force myself to do this when I'm especially busy but it's always worth it.

25 PRESENT MORE THAN ONE DESIGN SOLUTION. Often the first is the best one, but testing one or two others gives your client alternative options (your taste may be completely different from theirs), and forces you to more thoroughly test your preferred idea.

26 TALK THROUGH YOUR IDEA WITH A PRINTER BEFORE PRESENTING IT TO THE CLIENT. The printer will be able to tell you if there are any potential production problems (in which case you have to choose whether or not to take the risk), and may be able to offer some useful advice.

27 AS SOON AS THE CLIENT HAS AGREED ON THE FORMAT GET A FULL SPEC TO THE PRINTER. You need to be aware of any potential production restraints at the start.

28 DON'T BE A DUMMY. Always get a blank dummy produced and make sure the client sees it.

29 ALWAYS BE POLITE, PROFESSIONAL, AND RESPECTFUL TOWARDS YOUR CLIENT. A healthy client/designer relationship is key to a successful end product.

---

print details

Plymouth Arts Centre publication

general description:
80pp publication with separate cover

format (trim size):
210 x 280mm portrait

extent:
80pp + 4pp cover + 4pp half-width insert (See PDF)

colour:
cover: 2 spot outer, 1 spot inner (from 2 spot)
pp.1–10: 1 spot (black)
pp. 11–74: 4-col
pp.75–80: 1 spot (black)
4pp half-width insert (between pp. 44–45): 1 spot (black)

paper stock:
pp.1–10: 90gsm Cyclus Offset
pp.11–74: 120gsm gloss white (economical)
pp.65–80: 90gsm Cyclus Offset
4pp half-width insert (between pp. 44–45): 100gsm pink coloured copy paper – cheapest available

scans:
no scans

document format/version:
Adobe InDesign 5 (CS3)

30
Keep a record of all correspondence in case something goes wrong. Always agree on prices in writing, not over the phone where there is no visual record.

Anne Odling-Smee

www.o-sb.co.uk

Active as a graphic designer since 1996, when she graduated with a first from the course in Typography & Graphic Communication at Reading University. Anne Odling-Smee worked at design consultancy Esterson Lackersteen, then at August publishers before setting up O-SB design in 2001. Anne teaches at the University of Arts London, the Konstfack in Sweden, and has lectured at the Goethe Institut Krakow and Centre for Contemporary Art in Poland. She is author of *The New Handmade Graphics* (RotoVision, 2003). Her latest project, a catalog design for the prestigious Deutsche Börse Photography Prize, was launched in conjunction with the exhibition opening. Featuring the works of the four short listed photographers, the books are beautifully bound in a rough textured stock with foil-blocked cover lines, and a choice of four photographs.

Autobahn

www.autobahn.nl

Maarten Dullemeijer, Rob Stolte, and Jeroen Breen make up Autobahn. After graduating from Hogeschool voor de Kunsten Utrecht, they have since worked as an independent graphic design office. Autobahn is inspired by everything. What they conceive and design is characterized by large gestures and a clear message. Authenticity and a remarkable signature are two important elements in their work. Typography with capital letters is often strikingly evident, and also bright colors, hidden jokes, humor, and reflection. Autobahn works for the cultural and social sectors and for some commercial customers, preferring to take part in the creative process as early as possible. This would be ideally in the form of critical thinking and as a full partner. They are firm believers that a team will always have a greater (creative) network to appeal to.

31 Clients are out there. We usually envision working with someone who has excellent knowledge of the problem at hand, and is not easily satisfied, knows how designers work, and is willing to listen to our advice, so that together we can create something that fits the solution to the problem. They should be willing and able to pay what design is worth.

32 We always make clippings of things we find on the Internet or in magazines related to the briefing. With these clippings we visualize the briefing's visual range. After that we design a small leaflet in which we show the client which steps we took to come up with the final idea and form.

33 Read a book on semiotics. Semiotics is divided into three categories:
1. Semantics, or the relation between signs and the things they refer to, their *denotata*.
2. Syntactics, or the relation of signs to each other in formal structures.
3. Pragmatics, or the relation of signs to their impacts on those who use them.
I think every graphic designer (or any other artist for that matter) should have at least some knowledge of semiotics. Otherwise it's impossible to define your own work.

34 Always plan a meeting on Monday morning to review the week ahead. For example, during this meeting we divide assignments, get rid of possible frustrations, and leave with everybody knowing what to do and what the others are doing.

36 Have external creative sessions. Autobahn likes to take part in creative sessions. To devise, develop, and achieve ideas together is one of the best aspects of creative entrepreneurship. Meeting with creative people with new visions is a big plus. We have, for these reasons, initiated Blue Monday—a weekly opportunity for anyone with inspiration to brainstorm with us in our studio. It includes lunch and a game of football (providing there is good weather).

37 We prefer to create a friendly environment for our clients. But there must always be space to be serious and a place for critical remarks.

38 Wear your everyday clothes. Don't do suits!

39 Have a website to give to people after the first contact. Sometimes a potential client wants to have a meeting, and we bring some work that we can discuss. A big no-no is to bring a portfolio map! With this, you tend to present finished projects, while the sketches are just as interesting to talk about. Just bring your work in a shoebox or try to find a way for your presentation that expresses your work or the way you work. By doing this, you'll already stand out in the crowd!

35
Always brainstorm with your team before starting an assignment. We try to break out of the daily routine before we start the brainstorm session. This enhances creativity. So sometimes we just go outside or do something fun. After that, the mind is empty and it allows you to focus on the task at hand. Usually we hang large pieces of paper on the walls and start writing down everything that comes to mind. No idea is too crazy or expensive. Later, ideas are combined into two or three directions from which the concept is created. Then we check if the idea fits the budget. We think that if you start thinking about the money and feasibility, you slow down the brainstorm and possibly discard a lot of good ideas.

40 Love to work with your hands, though not every assignment is suitable for that method. We always try to come up with a (form) solution that fits the assignment. Otherwise it just becomes a trick you repeat time after time. I think our leitmotif is that we want the receiver of our design to participate in that design. We want to see how far the receiver would go to simply cross something out on a flyer or poster, or go through complex paths in a book to reveal the message. There is a lot of interactivity in our designs.

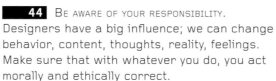

41 THINK BEFORE YOU START. When I get briefed to a new project, I usually take some time to think about it; I'll work on other assignments but will have the new task in the back of my head. This helps me to understand the project, so I can then run through concepts, ideas, or visualizations in my head. Often, before I actually start designing I already know what the result or the technique is going to look like.

42 CHALLENGE YOURSELF. For me it is important to take any project to the next level. I try to make myself think of ways and solutions that are new to me and/or never seen before. I push myself by hardly ever being satisfied with my work—it takes days or weeks before I can see the quality in whatever work I have done. Maybe this is because I always think there must be a better, smarter, or prettier solution.

43 BE AUTHENTIC. All the influences that surround us everyday make it difficult for us to walk our own lines. For me it is most important to be myself, create my own style, my thoughts and my way to find solutions. Being influenced by other work is normal; but only by taking this influence, with your thoughts and ideas aligned to the specifics of your projects, will you create something authentic.

44 BE AWARE OF YOUR RESPONSIBILITY. Designers have a big influence; we can change behavior, content, thoughts, reality, feelings. Make sure that with whatever you do, you act morally and ethically correct.

45 EXPERIMENT. Trial and error is the best way to find out if your idea works or not. Make dummies, scribble, test it on people, print it big, paint it, try different materials, and different techniques. Only by trying will you find out. The best about experiments is that you will probably end up with something that you couldn't think of before. And it's fun.

WIR SUCHEN PFADFINDER, MASO- CHISTEN UND ERBSEN- ZÄHLER.

AM BESTEN IN EINER PERSON. WW.DIE- UNBESTECH- LICHEN.DE

46 EDUCATE YOURSELF, BE OPEN MINDED, LOOK AT AS MANY THINGS AS YOU CAN, GO THROUGH YOUR STREETS AND LIFE WITH OPEN EYES, TRAVEL A LOT. I have always been interested in the unknown and if I don't know something I want to learn it and know about it. By experiencing the unknown you will get a better understanding of things. This expands your horizon and consequently betters your work.

47 FINDING IDEAS. There are many ways to find ideas. I tend to play through ideas in my head, cross out the easy and obvious solutions and then try to narrow it down to the point from an unexpected angle. Thinking outside the box creates interesting results that might have more depth, double meaning, or usability.

48 RECORD YOUR THOUGHTS. Some people have diaries, others sketchbooks or to-do-lists. I am a list person, I write down everything that I want to try. In my studio I pin all those ideas and scribbles to a wall. This helps me to not forget and it's a great research board for ideas. Many times it has helped me to find an idea or direction for a project.

49 FREE YOURSELF. By being free and independent you can follow your dreams and wishes. A free mind and spirit is good for creativity. Love life, nature, animals, people, yourself, and what you do.

50 Be critical with yourself, your environment, and your work. This will drive you to the next level.

Axel Peemöller

www.axelpeemoeller.com

Hamburg's own Axel Peemöller has been drawing, painting, and designing ever since he was able to hold a pencil in his hand. He started at the Universität Düsseldorf, then in Hamburg, and finally in Swinburn, Melbourne, where he attended and received a masters by research. It's evident through his works that design is not simply a job for him but it occupies his life with passion. Through the years he has lived in different countries and worked for companies all around the globe. Working for studios and clients as a contractor or freelancer, he never misses a chance to contribute to design. Some of his most recent projects are: a new corporate identity and website for Sevim Aslan Photography, illustrations for the *Feld* magazine literature section, and identity concepts for the motion graphic studio Sehsucht.

BarfootWorldwide

www.barfootworldwide.com

Jeff Barfoot is founder and principal of the design studio BarfootWorldwide, and is also Design Director of CommerceHouse (an advertising agency) in Dallas. His design and illustration work has been recognized by The Art Directors Club of New York, *Communication Arts*, *Graphis*, *Print* magazine, the *AR100* (for Annual Report design), The Dallas Society of Visual Communications, The American Institute of Graphic Arts, and The American Advertising Federation. He is past editor in chief of *Rough Magazine*. Jeff has also served on the board of directors of the Dallas/ Fort Worth chapter of AIGA. He is very proud to be the cofounder of the National Student Show & Conference, the nation's largest creative competition and conference designed for communication arts students, now in its fifth year.

51 BRIEF > IDEAS > SKETCH. Once the creative brief is written (which we make as short as possible, so our goals for the project stay clear), we read it over, and then walk away from it. After a few days—we can't quite describe how—we find that we've been thinking about it off and on in the back of our minds. When we sit down to sketch, we almost always find that we have a few ideas that seem to pour out of the pen.

52 SKETCH > PAPER > PENCIL. We always, always, always sketch first. And that is a loose term—our preliminary sketches are a combination of words and images that we feel can help solve the problem. At first, these ideas are not complete thoughts: we could have a tagline we like, an illustration treatment that feels appropriate, some image concepts. We then put these pieces together to form larger, more cohesive ideas. Once we have several of these more complete ideas we critique them, removing some, combining some, to arrive at the fewest number of strong ideas. Whenever possible, this is what we show to a client. Showing pencils helps ensure that the client will choose a direction based on the idea, and not based on periphery considerations like "Oooh, I love that color!", which can be much more subjective. Once the client approves the overall concept in sketch form, we move to comps, and then final layout. We really try to keep the spontaneity and freshness of the sketches alive in the comps, tying to keep them as close to the pencils as possible (unless we have a different, better idea along the way).

53 LIBRARY > BOOKS > RESEARCH. We always do research, but not too much. We have found that research and information can be as dangerous as it can be helpful. We strongly feel that there is a fine line between not doing enough research and doing too much. Of course, it is helpful to research our subject matter and what the potential competitors for our project will be. But doing too much research can sometimes cause a sort of information overload, and can cause a designer to lose sight of the original goal for the project.

54 CLUTTER > CHAOS > WORKING SPACE. A chaotic, cluttered working space seems counter-productive, but we find that having a workspace with a lot going on is healthy. Having several projects going at once in different stages is really good for our thought process. For us, focusing on one project at a time isn't nearly as productive as jumping from project to project. We think it keeps our brains active, keeps us from getting too bogged down or even stuck on one project. The other benefit is that a cross-pollination of ideas starts to take place, where an aspect of one project might spark an idea for another.

55 SUBCONSCIOUS > INPUT > INSPIRATION. We have a very strong opinion regarding inspiration: we think that enjoying and experiencing these things is where ideas come from in the first place. We have put some thought into this, actually, and we think that the best ideas are a combination of smaller things (words, visuals, etc.) that are put together in a way that is unexpected, and with luck, are something no one has ever thought of before. But in order to do this, a designer must experience as many things, and as many different things, as possible. What this does is build an arsenal or library of sorts in your subconscious, so when you sit down to a concept on a project, your mind can pull all of these parts together to form ideas. Because of this, we strongly feel that the more input you give your mind to work with, the greater the output will be.

Home 4 - yard / exterior related

Chapter 2: Get Your Kids Involved

Home 4 - yard / exterior related

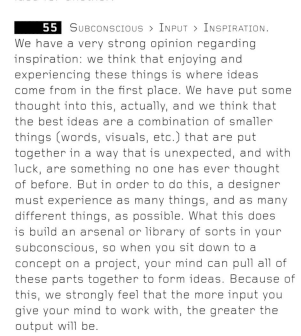

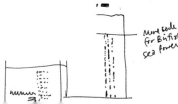

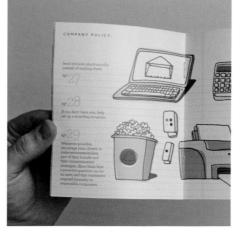

57 CHALLENGES > REWARDS > CLIENTS. There is no ideal client, but that's the best thing about what we do. If every client let you do everything you wanted, what fun would that be? Solving each client's needs and challenges in the most creative way possible is the most rewarding thing we do. If what we come up with wins a few design awards or appears in a few annuals, we are all the more excited. But again, if that happened every time, the joy of that would be gone.

58 REFERRALS > AWARDS > NEW PROJECTS. Almost every job we have worked on (so far) has come as a referral from an existing client or friend of the studio (printers, paper suppliers, etc.). We try very hard to maintain our reputation of doing strong creative and being pleasant people to work with. Occasionally, we will get a new project from a client who sees our work in an annual or sees our work out in the world and takes the time to find out who was behind it. We try very hard to give our clients both the best work and the best experience, and the rest has taken care of itself.

59 STYLE > CLIENT NEEDS > TECHNIQUES. We think that in order for each idea to be as strong as possible, each technique used on each project should be dictated by the needs of that project, and support the overall goal or concept. We abhor design studios that claim or practice a "style." We think this a huge disservice to clients. Each client is unique, and has unique needs and goals; forcing a look on them that a designer thinks is "cool" or "our studio's style" is just plain wrong.

60 TEAM EFFORT > QUALITY CONTROL > PRODUCTION CONTROL. We try very hard to be as collaborative as possible, so we have the most ideas and quality control on our projects. Although each project has a Project Lead, we try to stay involved as a group, starting with the first conception of ideas, all the way to production, printing, or programming.

56
MADNESS > DARKNESS > OPTIMISM. If there is a leitmotif in our work, we like to think it's optimism. The world has enough madness and darkness in it. We try, whenever possible, to design things that add a little light and cheerfulness.

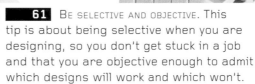

61 BE SELECTIVE AND OBJECTIVE. This tip is about being selective when you are designing, so you don't get stuck in a job and that you are objective enough to admit which designs will work and which won't.

62 DIVERSIFY. Try to differentiate in style and the way you look at your work. Try to use different techniques and typefaces, don't become a "one trick pony."

63 LEARN FROM EVERYTHING AND EVERYONE. I think you can learn from every experience, even if it's negative.

64 BE MORE THAN A DESIGNER. Broaden your horizons. The best inspiration will come from other fields than design.

65 KEEP YOUR FRIENDS CLOSE BUT YOUR CRITICS CLOSER. It's nice that people like your work but you can actually learn much more from people who make valid criticism.

Keep your friends close but your critics closer.

BE MORE THAN A DESIGNER.

YOU ARE ONLY GOING TO DIE FROM YOUR OWN ARROGANCE.

66 NEVER MAINTAIN A STATUS QUO. This one is about how you perceive a client or a job. Never try to stereotype a client in a certain kind of field. Always think there is more you can do for him or her.

67 LOVE WHAT YOU DO. Never let the passion go out of your work. Don't become a malcontent, even when its not going good at your workplace or you have a burn out. Just trust your work and everything will sort itself out.

68 HELP YOUR FELLOW DESIGNER. This is more about helping people out with techniques, advice, and even with deadlines. For me as a designer, you also have the responsibility to help where you can, like Spiderman.

69 ALWAYS QUESTION PEOPLE WHO WANT TO TEACH YOU SOMETHING. Well this one is about killing your darlings. It's great to learn something from other designers, books, lectures, but always question if the advice is fitting for you. Maybe you would do better in going the totally opposite direction.

HELP YOUR FELLOW DESIGNER

70 YOU ARE ONLY GOING TO DIE FROM YOUR OWN ARROGANCE. Always try to avoid arrogance, because the quality of your work will come to a standstill. And hell! Nobody will have coffee with you anymore.

Bart Kiggen
www.kiggen.be

A Belgian graphic designer and artist, he received a Master of Arts in Graphic and Advertising Design at Antwerp's Koninklijke Academie voor Schone Kunsten in 2004 before pursuing a career in graphic design. Currently active as a freelancer under the name Kiggen in a variety of fields ranging from identity work, motion design and pretty much anything he can get his hands on. Being a freelancer, he has the freedom of working for any kind of client in any kind of field. A huge fan of work pauses, when not at his desk he can usually be found drinking coffee in the Cafénation. Some of his recent projects include: the Leasense Blend restyling, identity for fashion designer Gunyho Kim, packaging designs for Schwarzkopf, and the identity and animations for Nordic Fire.

Bendita Gloria

www.benditagloria.com

Alba Rosell and Santi Fuster run Bendita Gloria, a small graphic design studio in Barcelona. The studio is focused on editorial design, packaging, branding, and art direction, and offers design solutions based on a conceptual approach to each project. They are both graphic designers and talented graphic arts specialists. Alba has recently been granted a R+FAD scholarship to research and expand on special bookbinding systems. Some of their recent projects include: Guiu Bosch's unfinished and rejected illustrations catalog—consisting of a folder in which the author can add new material and comments (printed in post-its) as well, and posters for a Stevie Wonder's tribute party—the juxtaposed song titles and its translation into braille, identified with the musician.

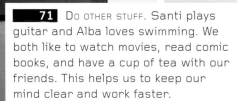

C'MON CALL US

71 DO OTHER STUFF. Santi plays guitar and Alba loves swimming. We both like to watch movies, read comic books, and have a cup of tea with our friends. This helps us to keep our mind clear and work faster.

72 DECORATE, TIDY UP. Many things hang on the walls of our small studio. It's located in a penthouse in Barcelona and iTunes is always running. It's very important for us to keep it nice and orderly.

73 KEEP IT ORGANIZED. Gmail + Google calendar + post-it notes. That's a combination!

74 KNOW WHO YOU'RE WORKING FOR. You should design for anyone who is highly motivated and open minded.

75 STAY OFF THE WEB. We love print design and we like to mix it with plenty of craft techniques.

76   SCREEN-PRINT. We are very interested in modern screen-printing. Many materials can be printed and there are some impressive effects, like foam or glow-in-the-dark ink, to play with.

77   HAND-MAKE. Graphic design with a certain hand-made feeling—when justified—looks great.

78   IT'S IMPORTANT TO WORK WITH GOOD PRINTERS. Arts Gràfiques Orient in Barcelona are both that and really nice people.

79   LURE YOUR CLIENTS. Usually we design something three-dimensional (a book, a postcard, or whatever) that brings people to our website, where our work can be seen.

80
AVOID INDIFFERENCE. Everything should be personal and dissimilar. The worst scenario for a client is to go unnoticed.

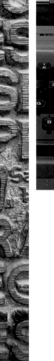

81 IDEAS LIE EVERYWHERE. While thinking of a simple logo design that would be able to express both the element of water and that of man made artifacts, I came across this picture that combined all elements perfectly.

82 CHOOSE COLORS WISELY. Good (logo) design must work both in colors and in black and white. It's best to limit colors often using monochromatic solutions, playing with empty and fill spaces.

83 FORM FOLLOWS FUNCTION. Knowing the subject of your design is of fundamental importance. But research in terms of stylistic options tends to be distracting. Abstraction from design is a better way to be original.

84 DOODLE > DIGITAL > RATIONALIZATION. Start with the least limitations, freehand doodling, on paper, on a napkin, or on a wall, is perfect at the beginning of the creative process. Once the idea is found then you can move on to digital production, and start thinking of grids, to optimize and rationalize the entire structure of the project.

85 FONTS AND CUSTOMIZATION. Fonts must be chosen to add contrast, or to balance graphic weights in a composition. It's also useful to customize fonts to add effects and follow the general idea of a project.

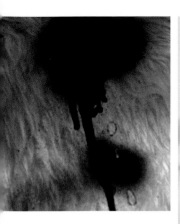

86 CHAOS IS THE ESSENCE OF CREATIVITY. I could never work in an orderly environment. Disorder is movement, movement is energy. It's important to "assimilate" the workplace, it's difficult to feel comfortable right away in a new place.

87 FAVORITE TECHNIQUES. When I realize something for a non corporate client, I enjoy mixing medias and techniques to achieve an uncommon feel. I really believe in the effects born from very different ingredients. When you have to be a designer—and not an artist—then you should really need to adapt to the client's needs. It's more of a matter of right or wrong rather than of personal aesthetics.

88 WORK AS IF YOU HAD HALF THE TIME. Never underestimate your workload! By working as if I had half the time to do it I usually avoid missing deadlines and manage last-minute inconveniences and heart attacks. I have noticed that an estimate of an hour work usually triples.

89 WRITE IT DOWN. Keep a paper agenda, old school rocks!

90 FOLLOW HERACLITUS'S MOTTO: "THE SUN IS NEW EVERY DAY."

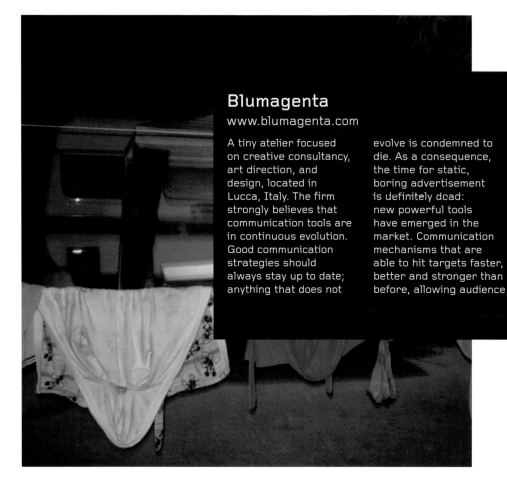

Blumagenta
www.blumagenta.com

A tiny atelier focused on creative consultancy, art direction, and design, located in Lucca, Italy. The firm strongly believes that communication tools are in continuous evolution. Good communication strategies should always stay up to date; anything that does not evolve is condemned to die. As a consequence, the time for static, boring advertisement is definitely dead: new powerful tools have emerged in the market. Communication mechanisms that are able to hit targets faster, better and stronger than before, allowing audience interaction and creating a solid link between product, consumer and brand. Blumagenta like to think of themselves as people who are able to think creatively at 360 degrees. And an outsider might judge that thinking out of the box is really their specialty.

Bob Faust

www.faustltd.com

Son, brother, cousin, uncle, godfather, husband, dad, boss, and friend-as-needed. Doer, dreamer, developer, teacher, typographer, tax-payer, listener, leader, and lover-of-stuff. Designer from Chicago. The studio is located in beautiful Riverside, Illinois. Faust loves tacos, smoothies, swimming, pedaling, paddling, and Stella. Most importantly (and probably why he's here), he's an experienced and successful graphic designer. His abilities lie in print and web design, specializing in important cultural clients like the University of Illinois at Urbana-Champaign, the Brookfield Zoo, Tootsie Roll Industries, McDonald's Corporation, Playboy Enterprises, Chicago Public Radio, Illinois Arts Alliance, and the Museum of Contemporary Art Chicago.

91 TAKE ADVANTAGE OF MOMENTUM. Put as much creative thinking as possible down on paper immediately after a kickoff meeting.

92 EAT WITH YOUR IDEAS. Slow down and live with your ideas outside the studio. Imagine how it will be used in as many situations as possible.

93 PUMP IRON. Get away from the computer and do something for your body.

94 TAKE ADVANTAGE OF TiVo. Get your reality TV quota in half the time, and give your brain a break.

95 BE YOURSELF...but yourself in their world. Know your potential clients' culture and position yourself accordingly.

96 USE ALL YOUR TOOLS. The form a brochure takes, the process you print with, the substrate you print on, etc. All need be considered early on. Contrary to public opinion it is not all about the font.

97 CHRISTIE BRINKLEY'S MOLE. We all know beauty is in the eye of the beholder and familiarity breeds desire, so give an unfamiliar font a try. With enough time and experimentation you may find the things you were uncomfortable with are the things you enjoy most.

98 DUMP THE DESIGN ANNUALS. They are great for our egos and to go through once, but don't use them as a reference tool. Find your true inspirations outside our own industry.

99 Listen to yourself...not me. :)

100 MAKE FRIENDS OF YOUR CLIENTS. Really knowing and enjoying each other makes solving their problems easier and getting their approval way easier.

101 TAKE THE LONG ROUTE TO WORK. It helps to think when generating ideas. After a client briefing we take the long route back to work via a park, a coffee shop, or anywhere else that seems like a nice place to talk and think.

102 MATERIALIZE YOUR IDEAS FIRST. Doodle in sketchbooks, go straight to the computer, or produce a mock-up. Mock-ups are good, because they show things you hadn't thought of. Carry these around with you in your bag for a while, it helps you get a feeling for the project, and to understand it better.

103 WARNING! CREATIVITY HAS BEEN PROVED TO BE ENHANCED BY: listening to country music, going to the opera, having pub talks, reading comics, gazing out of bus windows, cooking, waiting in the post office queue, eating large quantities of red meat.

104 WORKING SPACE COSMOLOGY. Four tables with computers, one table with a cutting board and guillotine, one table with a kettle and a mini fridge, a table with a laser and inkjet, and a table with buttery biscuits and bananas. One likes chaos. The other likes some kind of structure to the chaos. All in all we would prefer having separate universes in order to achieve this.

105 IT'S ALL ABOUT REFERENCES. By doing good work, you promote your work. Sometimes we try cold calls for the fun of being totally annoyed and frustrated after three tries.

PRIVATE GARDEN
NO DOGS
NO CYCLING
NO BALL GAMES
NO MUSIC
NO VANDALISM
OBSERVE GARDEN RULES

106 LOOK LIKE YOU SHOULD LOOK. We used to wear suits sometimes, but I think we disappointed clients like that, as they expect the creatives to come up looking all casual. Now, we'd usually dress smartish, but not overdress.

107 COMMUNICATE. Use a mobile phone, switch it on, don't rely on telepathy.

108 FONTS. DO'S AND DON'TS. Do's: Akzidenz Grotesk, Sabon, Univers. Don'ts: Rotis Semi-Serif, Avant Garde, and about 200,000 other useless and ugly fonts.

109 HAVE A FAVORITE PRINTSHOP. Follow our projects through until they're finished. We mainly print with Offizin Sheufele in Stuttgart.

110
GRIDS ARE YOUR FRIENDS.

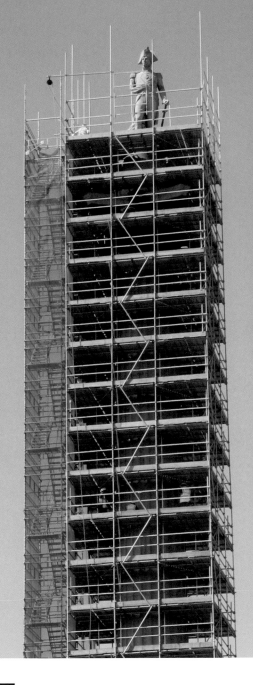

Brighten the Corners

www.brightenthecorners.com

Established in 1999, it is a small organization that handles both large and small-scale projects. Whether designing a book, a stamp, or branding an organization, they believe that communication should be clear and direct, and that good design always makes a difference. Brighten the eCorners in an independent, multi-disciplined design and strategy consultancy with offices in London and Stuttgart. This internationality also shows in their rich and textured work that spans from smart, functional website design to diverse but always cutting edge editorial design.

In this field they have established a name for themselves, having worked for Arnoldsche Art Publishers, Merrel Publishers, and being shortlisted for the Stiftung Deutshe Buckhunst (Most Beautiful Book Award 2004)

Bunch

www.bunchdesign.com

The agency was established in 2002 by Denis Kovac and Paulo Silva. It spread organically from London to Zagreb and then to Singapore. Talented friends joined, and the union formed the multi-disciplinary design practice that is the Bunch of today.

Bunch uses their wide range of specializations to create intelligent and consistent brands for diverse clients. As designers they believe that creativity, clarity, and consistency are the keys to successful design. Some of their latest projects include an identity for Institut

Parfumeur Flores, work for 55DSL, HBO, MTV as well as the BBC and Nike's retail design for the launch of their new Windrunner metallic range, including in-store graphics and point of sale displays as well as retail layouts.

111 IDEA-GENESIS. This is a combination of sitting, pacing, strolling, scribbling, head rubbing, pencil chewing, and paper throwing, really. Quite often reading the brief then sleeping on it helps. When the mind is relaxed ideas seem to come a bit easier.

112 TRY TO REACH THE "EUREKA MOMENT." Depending on what the idea is and where I am, I may need to photograph something on my phone, or doodle on a napkin or leave myself a voice mail. All depends on when the "eureka moment" happens. But it all begins in the mind, then spreads out to whatever medium I have close to hand. Then that may translate to the computer for development, depending on the needs of the idea.

113 PROJECT ACQUISITION IS A COMBINATION OF GENTLE PRODDING AND UNASHAMED BEGGING. It's a balance of reminding your existing clients you're still there, you're still brilliant at what you do, whilst chasing that new piece of new business to raise your profile or open doors to new industries. With new clients, I find that it's good to set up a face-to-face meeting. They'll remember you in that way. But you have to maintain client relationships by e-mailing and calling occasionally, without being intrusive.

114 THERE'S A TIME AND PLACE FOR BEING BOTH SERIOUS AND FRIENDLY. It's easy enough to be friendly at the start of a project, but as the deadline edges closer, the work days get longer, and the client's requests seem more like demands, it's so much harder to maintain that same level of friendliness. If a client is being unreasonable then it's important to don your serious face and stand up to them. But then finish with a smile.

115 ANY ACTIVITY OUTSIDE THE STUDIO STIMULATES CREATIVITY. Sleep is one of my favorite pastimes and research has shown that it definitely aids the creative thought process. But on a more serious note, our ideas are unique to us because of our own individual experiences and preferences. That's why no two designers would ever come up with exactly the same solution to a brief. It's incredibly important to have a good work/life balance so that both sides can feed off each other.

116 KEEP CONNECTED. If only it could be possible by means of tin can and string! The global nature of Bunch has meant relying on the Internet to communicate. MSN, iChat, Skype— all play a big part in the way we communicate with each other. We work between London, Zagreb, and Singapore so instant messaging is incredibly important in our day-to-day work. Video calling is great, as you do tend to miss the sight of your colleagues in the other studios too.

117 USE 'EM, DON'T ABUSE 'EM. Plug-ins and add-ons can be great but lots of designers can get a bit obsessed with a new one they've just discovered. I try to be aware of what's going on in that world, but not to rely on it.

118 HAVE A FAVORITE PRINTER. For us it's Kratis. They're simply amazing. We're a bit biased as they're now our friends, but they really do know their business inside and out.

119 PRESENTING YOUR WORK. We have the conventional digital forms of website and PDFs. But we don't really print our portfolio in the usual way. Since we started, we've had books as our portfolio. *Chapter 1*, as we called it, was a slim volume printed in 2005. We used to take it to new clients so they had a physical Bunch presence in their office once we'd left. *Chapter 2* was a much more ambitious venture, at least four times as thick with multi-colored spines. They're great to have as its lovely to flick through and see how far we've journeyed.

120 IT'S ALL VERY SIMPLE. You begin with a great idea. And then you execute the hell out of it. When you look at any great piece of design, there is something quite wonderful about it that you can't quite place. It's not one specific element, but more the whole. The concept, the execution, the finite detail within that binds the whole piece to strike a careful balance between form and function.

121 READ. Anything on Chinese landscape painting. Amazing stuff.

122 PUT EVERYTHING IN WRITING. E-mail, e-mail, e-mail...your best friend.

123 IF YOU'RE WORKING HARD, GO TO LUNCH. It's good to take a break, get out, and get recharged.

124 GET A GOOD PRINTER. Have a good and fast printer for quick tests.

125 LOOK BEHIND YOU. "Always look behind you." I was once told by a photographer that when he shoots, after getting what he wants, he turns around. Because often what's going on behind him is just as interesting if not more than what's in front of him. I think it applies to design very well.

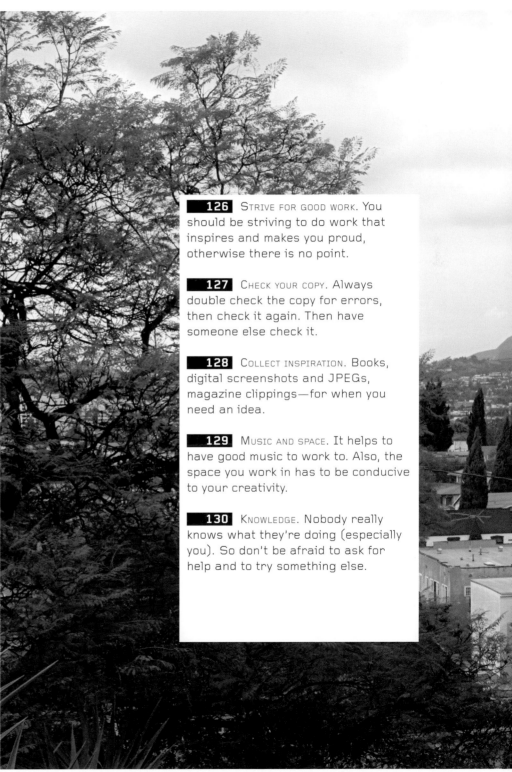

126 STRIVE FOR GOOD WORK. You should be striving to do work that inspires and makes you proud, otherwise there is no point.

127 CHECK YOUR COPY. Always double check the copy for errors, then check it again. Then have someone else check it.

128 COLLECT INSPIRATION. Books, digital screenshots and JPEGs, magazine clippings—for when you need an idea.

129 MUSIC AND SPACE. It helps to have good music to work to. Also, the space you work in has to be conducive to your creativity.

130 KNOWLEDGE. Nobody really knows what they're doing (especially you). So don't be afraid to ask for help and to try something else.

Carlos Tarrats

www.carlostarrats.com

Carlos Tarrats is a graphic designer based out of Los Angeles. After graduating in Art and Design at the University of California, Santa Barbara and at the Art Center College of Design, Carlos went on to work for American Apparel for two years after a freelancing career. His activities are not limited to graphic design, though. He is also a talented photographer specializing in black and white prints and independent art projects. Choosing medium over large format, this cross-pollinating designer/ artist has the freedom to move around the set much more easily while still maintaining an excellent negative size. His work comprises endless adjustments— back and forth in the composing and adjusting of the set in response to what's in front of the lens. Carlos Tarrats has been a featured artist at Susan Spiritus Gallery, California and Gallery Imperato, Maryland.

Chris Ro

www.adearfriend.com

Originally from Seattle, Washington, Chris finds very much delight in all that can be classified as extremely complex yet ultimately, very simple. He enjoys the occasional blending of two dimensions with three dimensions. Currently on a quest to find that which is that, you may find Chris in great love with fine typography, tinkering with some experimental photography or consuming the West coast burrito. Prior to his graduate studies, Chris held posts at a healthy handful of international design studios: ATTIK in San Francisco, New York and Leeds, Fork Unstable Media in Hamburg and Berlin and Fluid in San Francisco. Chris holds an undergraduate degree in Architecture from UC Berkeley. Chris is also a member of the AIGA. In his spare time, he's also a contributor for the graphic design journal *GraphicHug*™.

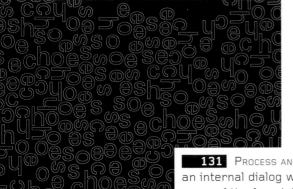

Happiness™

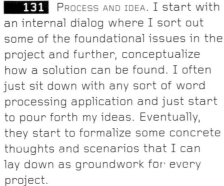

131 PROCESS AND IDEA. I start with an internal dialog where I sort out some of the foundational issues in the project and further, conceptualize how a solution can be found. I often just sit down with any sort of word processing application and just start to pour forth my ideas. Eventually, they start to formalize some concrete thoughts and scenarios that I can lay down as groundwork for every project.

132 SKETCH AND WRITE. I begin to just do some quick sketches to apply some visual language on some of this writing. Whether it be just a quick idea, or something that is lingering in my mind in terms of feel, I try to put it down. I think it is in this unison, where both written thoughts and visual thoughts meld, where any project begins to take some shape.

133 VISIONS VERSUS CLIENTS. I think my ideal client would be somebody who could see happiness. As designers, we often pour ourselves into projects. We truly get engrossed in the process and actually put our

hearts into it. We get lost in the making. We find ourselves at home in a moment of discovery. And I often wish clients could see this.

134 ORDER VERSUS CHAOS. I think I am internally torn by the same components. I have a practical, pragmatic side that sees only the logical solution in it all. But I feel that any logical solution needs an irrational side; something that is reflective of you inside the project. Otherwise, the project could have been done by anybody else. It is only when you are able to give yourself to a project that it can take a life of its own.

135 BALANCE AND STIMULATION. Testing that balance between just enough organization and just enough chaos to keep things fluid. So that, at any given point, I can find what I am looking for. But it is never too far from my reach and it is never too much to stifle any creativity. Just enough visual stimulation and clutter to go with a sensible organization.

136 SERIOUS VERSUS FRIENDLY. An interestingly contradictory scenario. And I wonder if the two can really be compared. For at heart, I know myself to be more friendly than serious. But when it comes to things dealing with businesses and folks investing in anything creative, I feel there is a serious side that needs to come out. Perhaps one that I am even less comfortable with.

137 DISCOVERY AND ITERATION. Pushing something, pushing a method, pushing a form to become something else. To see what else can happen with it. To see if it can be moved in another direction. I think I would liken this to sculpture in many ways.

138 SCREEN VERSUS PRINT. As much as I spend time and enjoy designing for interactive, I also miss the tactility of the print world. The nature of touching, feeling, and truly controlling an interaction with a printed piece. There is something that is so much more palpable in the sensory nature in interacting with a book, a print, or a craft. And it is this that I miss in the screen.

139 RESEARCH AND WAIT. Research only fuels a more informed and thorough solution or result. I'd say this takes place in tandem with the writing portion of a project. I'll look up materials, writings, other relevant data if it does inform the brief and inform the actual end result of the project. And it goes back and forth. I find something, write a bit about it. Then find something else and write some more. I think the best part of this process is the "a-ha" moment. The moment where you reach an epiphany and it triggers something internally.

140 GRIDS AND INTRICACIES. I love grids when they are broken. When they are stretched to capacity. When they let the intricacies of human nature pour in and define or undefine them.

141 Be patient.

142 Act gentle though straightforward.

143 Know what you can and can't do.

144 Go for a walk.

145 Go for a beer.

Did you mean: <u>to the **point**</u>

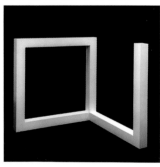

146 Be able to reason your design decisions (and if you can't, know that there is no point to your design).

147 Don't mind starting all over again.

148 Don't wait for people to do things for you (it will take more energy than doing it yourself).

149 Don't listen to me (but study thoroughly your idols).

150
Make it beautiful, meaningful, exciting, original, and simple!

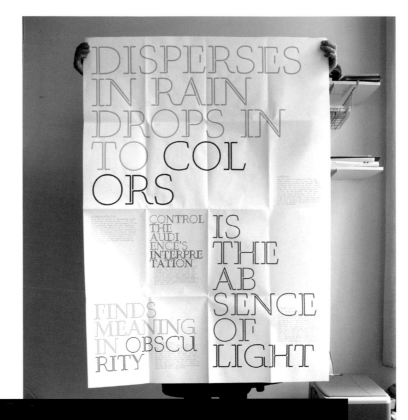

Claudia Doms

www.claudiadoms.com

Graphic design works in an associative way, and Claudia aspires to a form that takes a step aside from everyman's reading conventions. In her work, rules are self-set to generate source material for a possible outcome. These limitations are based on practical and theoretical research emerging from the project. They are not merely idea-generators but filters through which the form takes its ultimate shape. In this process-based design the final outcome unfolds itself rather than being generated. One of her latest projects where she showcases the result of this is Windsor and Woody Allen, an investigation on the unique connection between the famous filmmaker and the Windsor typeface. He has been using it since 1977 in his movie credits. The research was ultimately enriched with a three-way comparison with the drawings of Robert Crumb.

Clément Le Tulle-Neyret

www.printedmatter.fr

A well traveled and experienced young designer hailing from Lyon, France. He started to study graphic design very early on—he was only fifteen years old. Years later he attended the École Nationale des Beaux Arts de Lyon, where he graduated in graphic design. He then went on to gain international work experience at renowned studios like Value and Service in London, Mucho in Barcelona, Loran Stosskopf in Paris, finally going back to his own town and working for Trafik. He frequently uses typographic illustrations in his work, and does it with extreme heterogeneity of forms. During six months he carried on a fruitful collaboration with fellow designer Emmanuel Colomb leading them to be exhibited at the St. Étienne Design Biennal in 2008, Chop-Suey, Contacts, and What You See Is What You Get at Le Stand in Lyon.

151 Look around you.

152 Put yourself in everything you do.

153 Don't be shy.

154 Be honest.

155 Do only things you really want to do.

...or each
...tly
...being
...ntions of
...pired,
...municativ...

...ner-
...rked most of
...nce of his
...s on the cover,
...cut up
...o a simple
...direct graphic
...au's 99
...Passing over
...he contents list
...les,
...d 'Dream', with
..., demonstrates
...nt virtuosity.
...u's translator

"Leaping forward another forty years
or so, here's a very graphic demonstration
of lateral thinking from a project initiated
by the artist Ryan Gander. As an exercise in
relinquishing any æsthetic contr...
work, he asked around ten desig...
make posters for fictional event...

156 Never be too serious.

157 Be rigorous and practical.

158 Only work with strong rules.

159 Always follow rules.

160
No half-measures.

162 ILLUSTRATOR PLAYGROUND. An exercise that I find very helpful is to constantly keep an Adobe Illustrator file with vector elements, typefaces in progress, and experimentations. A digital file in which composition does not matter. What is useful about this ongoing process file is that you begin to see your visual language develop. This also enables you to quickly add and further develop design assets into projects.

163 MARK YOUR TERRITORY. Surround your work-space with images, cut-outs, process work, and materials that inspire you. Your studio is your sanctuary; this exercise should grow organically. I constantly update, paste, and write over materials that are on my studio wall.

164 RELEVANCE. Know what's out there. I keep an inspiration folder on my computer that I constantly update with images that I find on the net. There are numerous image bookmarking websites in existence that I pull images from on a daily basis. The objective of this exercise is to expand your exposure to visual culture in an international context.

165 SKETCH OVER. Buy a magazine of your interest and use it as a sketchbook. It is important to choose a magazine with content that you enjoy. The purpose of this exercise is to create a dialogue with the text of the magazine. Sketch over images, cross-out text, highlight text, collage...there are endless possibilities!

Pigxtras
The Harmony Korine Purple Book

161
FIND INSPIRATION ELSEWHERE. **Graphic design does not exist in a bubble!** Log-out of your computer and forget about client work, accounting, and studio management for a day. Buy tickets to the symphony, experience a live jazz performance, attend a fashion show, go skydiving, start a martial arts class. Add some spice to your life, in turn, your work will embody this sense of adventure.

66 CROSS-POLLINATION. Collaborate on a project with a colleague, a friend, or a contemporary. Do not limit yourself to people in your discipline! Collaborating with others has always proved to be an invaluable experience for me. This dynamic interplay will force you to remove yourself from your comfort zone and will expose you to different modes of thinking.

167 VISUAL ESSAYS. These can take the form of installations, posters, motion graphics, etc. This exercise is a mainstay of my creative process. Personally, my preference lies in posters and I usually do three to five posters as a series. As with many of my previous exercises; do not limit yourself, there are no rules or boundaries! This is not client work, think of it as personal development. This exercise will further develop a visual language unique to you. If approached with an open mind, the experience can be rewarding.

168 MATERIALITY/RE-APPROPRIATION. Find inspiration and creative departure points through the exploration of different materials. I take regular trips to specialty paper vendors and textile stores in an attempt to find materials that can be incorporated into my work. By re-appropriating the inherent context of the materials, another dimension is added to my projects

169 DESIGN A TYPEFACE. The development of a personal typeface (digital, hand-drawn, or with found objects) will greatly improve your technical and creative sensibilities. This action will also aid in the development of your personal visual language; you will also gain a greater respect for an art form that is largely taken for granted.

70 DEPARTURE POINT AND INTERTEXTUALITY. This exercise will force you to delve into the depths of other academic disciplines such as philosophy, critical theory, media studies, etc. This exercise begins with a preliminary passage of inquisition. The library and Internet are wonderful resources; research a disciplinary track that you have an affinity for. If you are serious about your studies; you will soon find an author who's voice ignites your passion. Find a text that is relevant to your personal value system. The manifestation of this exercise can take any form, such as a motion graphics piece, a sculpture... use your imagination! Hopefully this exercise will be the starting point for further investigation into the subject matter at hand and will spawn a comprehensive body of work. Never define the final product at the onset. This is a challenging exercise that will lead you into different directions. Allow your mind to wonder.

Loosely, this was the process used to create the context for a project called: *The Book of O*, a hand-made lookbook exploring Pauline Réage's text *The Story of O* The departure point was a study into tattoo art. Through reviewing the works of critical theorists such as Roland Barthes and T.S. Elliot I was thrown into directions I never thought possible. I soon began studying the writings of Adolf Loos and Geoffrey Galt Harpham, among others. The ideologies of these authors became intertwined in my own personal philosophy. Their voices are now part of my work through filiation—it is inescapable, their voices are inseparable from my own! *The Book of O* embodies this intertextual experience.

Colin Chow

www.heist-toronto.com

An independent bespoke art director and graphic designer currently residing in Toronto. After working as art director of The KDU headquarters in New York, Colin returned to Toronto armed with experience in the fashion, arts, and cultural markets. Named "Top Talent" by *IDN* magazine in May, Colin's work has been showcased in publications internationally. Upon his return to Toronto, he has teamed up with renowned illustrator, artist and twin brother, Chow Martin, in the creation of a multidisciplinary art direction and aesthetics experimentation studio HEIST-Toronto. The studio brings together creative minds; all of whom share a passion for finely crafted aesthetics—the mandate is to interrupt the visual and cultural landscape of Toronto by creating tailor made solutions for design conscious clients locally and worldwide.

Coralie Bickford-Smith
www.cb-smith.com

Senior cover designer at Penguin Books, Coralie Bickford-Smith has a lot of experience under her belt. She has created several acclaimed series designs for Penguin, including the Hardback Classics and the Gothic Horror series, both of which were selected to feature in the 2009 D&AD annual, and the Boys' Adventure series, which won the 2008 British Book Design and Production Award for Series Identity. Coralie studied Typography at Reading University and recently she has been sharing her experience with students at London College of Communication, encouraging a sense of play in the process of design. She has a love of all things typographic and textile-based, and can often be spotted day dreaming on London buses in search of new ideas. Much of her spare time is taken up by collecting books, reading books, and thinking about books.

171 FIRST THINGS FIRST. To start developing ideas for a project, I set up mood boards of visual ideas—texture, ornament, objects, colors—all inspired by themes from the stories or by the period, or just the atmosphere of the project. Ideas often come to me at the cinema; it seems that while I am watching a movie, some part of my brain is working out design problems.

172 INSPIRATION AND RESEARCH. In terms of formal research, The London Library and St. Brides printing library are great for immersing myself in the history of typography and bookbinding. I try to begin off the computer when possible, just going out and sourcing ideas, colors, and textures. For inspiration I cast my net as wide as possible—books, objects, websites, etc. I love interior design as inspiration—I'm always making notes of color combinations I see, as color is really important to me in my design. A big part of the process is getting away from the desk, going out and absorbing all sorts of visual information.

173 LOOK FOR VISUAL INTERACTIONS WITHIN YOUR PROJECT. For example, I designed a series of ten well-loved classics: cloth-bound, jacketless hardbacks with a single matt foil stamped into the cover. In this case, the interactions were more obvious than others in terms of their connection with the text. I'm very keen on *Crime and Punishment*. There's a nice tension between the rigidity of the lines and the deconstruction of the grid that makes for an interesting parallel with the breakdown of Raskolnikov's moral certainty. There's also a Russian influence on the design, though from a later period than the book.

174 ONE BIG VISUAL OVERLOAD. *The Art of Looking Sideways* by Alan Fletcher has given me an enormous amount of pleasure. It's the book I have picked up the most and there is still new stuff to see every time.

175 GO THE EXTRA MILE, PRODUCTIONWISE. Cloth-bound hardbacks with foil stamping are a particular love of mine. It's taken a lot of work with the printers over the years to get right, so it's really good to see that effort pay off. My first cloth-bound book (Hans Christian Andersen's *Fairy Tales*) has been in print since 2005, and last year's *Poems for Life* is on its sixth edition. Going the extra mile in terms of production can make commercial sense, and it led to the recent series of ten hardback classics.

.76 To grid or not to grid. For the Hardback Classics I had the grid quite quickly as this was how I was going to slot in the different ideas and retain a consistent series style. Dealing with titles and author names of different lengths needs careful consideration to make sure the series style remains consistent and confident. For anyone interested in learning more about grid systems, I would recommend Josef Müller-Brockmann's excellent book, *Grid Systems in Graphic Design: A Handbook for Graphic Artists, Typographers, and Exhibition Designers*.

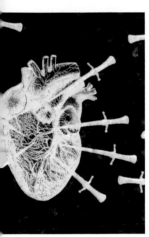

177 Colors. My design often has a limited color palate, consisting of only two colors. This has been a useful way of creating a strong series identity while allowing individual titles within a series to have their own color schemes. Blue and yellow combination is a current favorite of mine—I used it to design a horror book series. I like the way it breaks away from the colors conventionally associated with horror but still has the visual impact appropriate to the genre.

.78 Follow the project from start to finish. I try to go to the printers when I can and when it is a special project. In a publishing house you most likely have a production team that deals with the printers so you have to make sure you communicate well with them as they are the message carriers. I prefer speaking to printers face to face and seeing things on press, it enables a designer to keep more control over the final product.

179 Electronic versus real portfolios. As a designer I have an obsession to create beautiful, timeless artifacts for people to enjoy, cherish, and pass on. So when I present my work to clients, I like to be able to let them get to feel the real objects. This to me is much better than a PDF and it's my preferred choice. Obviously that isn't always practical, so websites and PDFs are invaluable and very important in getting work seen by a wider audience. If showing work electronically, I at least like to use photographs or scans that represent the physicality of the finished book.

YES

180

Stop designing, start playing. Recently I have been working on projects with students at London College of Communication with Wendy Chapple, passing on the principle that underpins my own work: "Stop designing, start playing." That philosophy is a way to get the students to free up their creative processes and really explore as widely as possible around a brief before focusing in on a particular solution. The temptation is always to take the constraints of the end product as a starting point as well as an end point, and that shuts off so many avenues of exploration. What Wendy and I are trying to encourage is a period of free association almost, of having fun with ideas and processes, and getting comfortable with the idea that, although 90% of what you produce in this period will be discarded, it will lead to places you wouldn't necessarily have reached directly, and the finished product will benefit as a result.

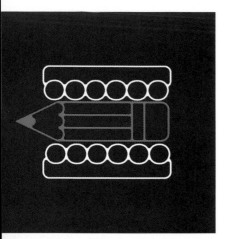

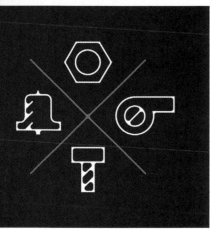

181 STAY HUNGRY LIKE BIGGIE ON HIS FIRST ALBUM. Success can satiate hunger and blur the line between confidence and laziness. It's best to remain critical and be open to the criticism of others. By staying hungry you prevent yourself from inhibiting your creativity. You'll not only continue to grow as a designer, but you'll keep things fresh and exciting for yourself. What kind of man would Bob Dylan be if he had just continued to do the same thing album after album? He would be Donovan I guess. And you *don't* want to be Donovan, man.

182 NUTS AND BOLTS VERSUS BELLS AND WHISTLES. It's not called breaking the rules when you don't know that you are—it's called making a mistake. Our buddy Modernism was nice enough to lay down some ground rules for us way back when and we are well-served to learn them and follow them, when appropriate. But at the same time, you did go to art school. Throw a couple lasers in there or something, dude.

183 CALL YOUR MOM. Just because she doesn't completely understand what you do for a living doesn't mean she doesn't want to hear about it.

184 SUCK IT, YOKO. There are two types of designers: Lennons and McCartneys. As a John Lennon, you create work that is message-driven, stark and serious, but you run the risk of seeming pretentious and/or naïve (in John Lennon's defense, he was unfortunately married to the world's worst art director). To be a Paul McCartney, on the other hand, means creating beautiful, meticulously crafted graphic design pop music, heavy on style but light on content. While either can be successful on its own (I love *Wings*), the best design employs both ideology and style (see popular music group *The Beatles*).

185 PRO BONO = GOOD ; U2 BONO = BAD. Do something for free! It will make you feel good and you'll have more creative control. Build your portfolio doing what you want to do. Employers can smell the creative musk of a portfolio grown with passion.

186
LISTEN TO POWERFUL 70S ROCK AND ROLL. Nothing makes me question the authenticity and integrity of my work like listening to Bruce Springsteen. Trust me—but if you don't trust me— then trust The Boss. I quit my first job out of school because I listened to my *Born to Run* LP every day after work, and I am much happier since. And now, on job applications, in the "Reason for leaving" section of my employment history, I can write: "Last chance power drive."

187 COPY. This is a dangerous idea, because, well, the world is already completely saturated with derivative horse-puckey created by knucklehead boner farmers with no taste. It's okay to bite another style, as long as you don't swallow the whole thing. Use it as a jump-off point and don't emulate it. Nobody is simply conjuring ideas out of ether and pixie dust. Be aware of your influences and use them to your advantage. If you have talent, intelligence, and integrity then your unique style will show through. I truly believe that.

188 EDIT EVERYTHING. Sometimes saying goodbye is the hardest part. Making something you love isn't nearly as difficult as letting it go.
An argument could be made that the real talent in design is to see and realize why something is ugly, not pretty. Designers, like the rest of the creative world, have a tendency to over think and over design. A more effective tactic is to find out what's not working and get rid of that. It's rough, but your mom never liked that one anyway.

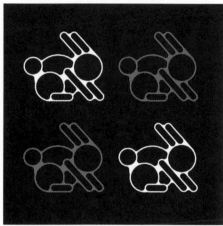

189 MINE THE DEPTHS OF YOUR COLD BLACK HEART. Graphic design isn't as dry and emotionless as it sounds when you explain it to girls in bars. If you get a visceral response to something you make then there's a good chance it will stir up similar feelings in other people too. Get those guts out as much as you can. If nothing else it will be interesting.

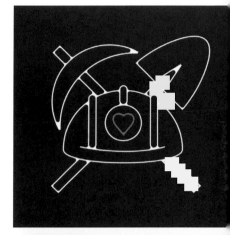

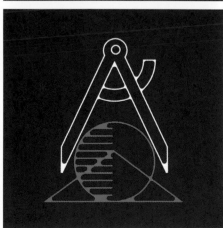

190 BE FREE TONIGHT. Unlike the controversial atmospheric electrical phenomena known as ball lightning, which can exist in a vacuum, design is married to commerce, and thus cannot. Being visually versed and technically proficient isn't enough to create successful engaging design. It demands that we draw upon history, pop culture, advertising, psychology, and a whole arsenal of non-design things to arm and inform our work. The best way to stock up is to get away from the computer and go out and live your life. Have some laughs, take a road trip, make out, barf on the subway platform, and throw something off a roof. Whatever it takes. Go out there, punch life in the neck, and steal its wallet.

Daniel Cassaro

www.youngjerks.com

A proud Long Island native, Daniel is a graduate of the School of Visual Arts. After finishing his studies, he moved on to start his career and now lives, works, and trips the light fantastic in Brooklyn. Young Jerks is his one-man design studio nestled in the heart of Williamsburg's adorable Italian neighborhood. When not working, Dan spends most of his time considering his Saturn Return and worrying about where he will take his Saturn out drinking when it gets here and if it will get along with his friends. His latest projects revolve around typography—his mechanical but warm McCartney typeface, an op-ed for the New York Times, an identity for Spacecraft boutique, a promotional CD for Bud Light Lime, and a type treatment-cover proposal for a short story by the talented Nik Ruckert.

Dmitry Galsan

www.iji-design.ru

For the last 30 years he has been living in the world of human beings, running the studio Iji and designing for both websites and print. A necessary psychedelic and unique style signs his work for corporate clients and most importantly self-initiated projects in the shade of the mountain Sumeru in the central part of Jambudv pa, waiting for the Nebu-chadnezzar DA203 to come and take him back to the Great Infinity. Nebuchadnezzar II was the first son, and successor, of Nabopolassar, who lead Babylon to its dependence from Assyria and left Nineveh in ruins. An attempted invasion of Egypt in 601 BC was met with drawbacks leading to numerous rebellions among the states of the Levant, including Judah. Encounters of the Third Kind are possible over the web. Only for the initiated.

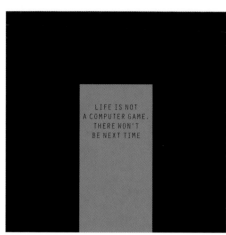

191 It's important: beauty is everywhere.

192 It's important: learn the rules in order to break them.

193 It's important: always work on a project as if it were your last.

194 It's important: don't overdo it.

195 It's important: travel to the places where you haven't been at least once a year.

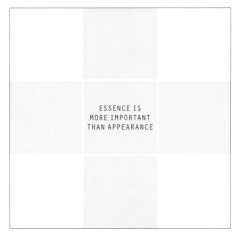

ESSENCE IS
MORE IMPORTANT
THAN APPEARANCE

THOUGH ALL THE
GOOD BOOKS ARE
ABOUT THE SAME
THINGS BOTH NOW
AND ALWAYS

WORKING
PLACES
1999–2009

MUSIC
IS THE BEST
DRUG

196 It's not important how you look. It's what you dream about.

197 It's not important if your working table is clean. Let your boss moan about it.

198 It's not important what you are listening to. It's what you hear.

199 It's not important which books you are reading. It's what you think.

200 It's not important what other people say and see. It's what you say and see.

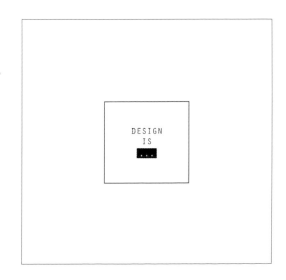

DESIGN
IS
....

201 Probably the best ideas come while in motion, outside of the studio.

202 Whether you prefer a notebook, many notebooks, new sheets or recycled paper, you should sketch on paper your first ideas.

203 It's important to recharge your creativity in any way suits you best: movies, cooking, outdoor sports...

204 Alternate design books with novels, for direct and indirect inspiration: Paul Rand/Italo Calvino/Bruno Munari/Thomas Glavinic.

205 Search new potential clients directly. The most important thing is to communicate with different people, creating relationships based on curiosity and trust.

207 Mix your techniques. Inks with pastels, collages and sketching with wax crayons. Adobe Illustrator, photos and vectors, a hammer and a handsaw.

208 Organize your timelines with a weekly progress meeting. It's easy, and most of the time you'll be able to prepare a timeline everyone can respect.

209 Try to digitalize your agenda, but if it doesn't work, the old paper-based agenda works fine.

210 The ideal client doesn't exist. Don't wait in vain. Nevertheless, he/she would respect your work, take part to the project, and give you a little of his/her time. Oh, and he/she would pay duly. It seems quite simple.

206
Each one learn one. Try to follow every step of the project, meet the printer and follow the printing process together.

Due mani non bastano

www.duemaninonbastano.it

Set in an old-style popular courtyard, a craftsman lab turned to a creative office. Due mani non bastano was founded in 2005 after many years of collaborations by Nicolò Bottarelli, Ilaria Faccioli and Davide Longaretti. They are three freelancers, working for publishers, advertisers, and any businesses that rely on visual communication forms. All of them are infused with the same passion to produce high quality images, to find the simplest and most elegant ways to communicate, to continue to innovate and experiment with materials, contents, and techniques, and to maintain a strong bond with nature. Brought together by mutual interest in image building, graphic design, and communication, they strive to develop creative solutions and provide support to clients with a great sense of enthusiasm and commitment.

El Studio

www.el-studio.co.uk

El Studio works in partnership with organizations that understand the importance of brand awareness and embrace the true value of creative, effective design solutions. The agency is in fact structured to work in collaboration with talented, like-minded individuals— designers, typographers, artists, writers, musicians, web/digital designers, architects, interior designers, photographers, make-up artists, marketing strategists that excel in their disciplines. This able mix of professions and talents has earned them a respectable list of clients such as Bailiwick Recording Co., Fife Regatta, Kshocolat, Dental White, Mark Seager, and Nicolson Maps. The latter has appointed El Studio to work in partnership in brand development; the initial project being to concentrate on the redesign and structure of their website.

Culture

211 Ideas and values of a people.

212 The stimulus of an idea.

213 Not narrow nor conservative in thought, expression, or attitude.

214 Creation of fundamental systems, maintaining flexibility.

Understand

215
PERCEIVE AND EXPLORE THE MEANING OF.

Inspiration

Progressive

Structure

Typography

Simplicity

Colour

Texture

Craft

216 The essence of language and communication.

217 Expression of emotion.

218 To reduce complexity.

219 Characteristics of a surface.

220 The technique, style, and artistry of working.

Once upon a time, there was....

221 ....there was a piece of wood

222 and some typography

223 a pinch of drawn writing

224 to see double

225 the written world

226 some plumed geometry

227 in the evening air

228 there were figures narrating

229 so

230 out there...

élitradesign

www.elitradesign.it

Roberta and Marco Sironi were born near Milan. Both studied at the Istituto d'Arte Monza and received a degree in Design and Aesthetics in Milan and Pavia. As well as graphic design and visual language, their research include writing about visual representation, about perceptibility, and about the plural ways in which they envision things. They are also lecturers in design in Milan and Alghero. élitradesign studio takes its name from the *elytra*, the protective cases that hedge some insects' wings while not in flight. In their idea, the graphic project is based on attention for the most understated tactile qualities, not only on the visual ones. élitradesign concentrates on the support material, on color shades, and on how the object develops into space while it is used.

Emmi Salonen

www.emmi.co.uk

Emmi is a graphic design practice based in London. Set up by Emmi Salonen in 2005, the studio specializes in designs for art, culture, commerce, academia, and organizations, using environmentally sound solutions whenever possible.

Whenever possible, Emmi uses recycled material, recycles and cycles. Emmi Salonen is originally from Finland. After studying Graphic Design in Brighton, where she graduated in 2001, she moved to Italy to work at Fabrica. Emmi went on to earn more professional

stripes back in London at Hoop and New York, where she worked with karlssonwilker inc. In 2005 she returned to London to set up her own studio. Emmi is also a session tutor at Ravensbourne University where she lectures regularly.

231 Set some time aside to reply to e-mails at certain intervals only during the day. For example, once in the morning, once in the afternoon. Otherwise your workflow gets interrupted continuously.

232 Plan your next day's schedule the day before. This way you can set on your tasks straight away and avoid the morning ponder.

233 Pay attention to the details; on layouts, mock-ups, presentations, everything. Then check these again.

234 Show your reasoning behind your designs, guide your client through the design.

235 When you look for work and go for interviews, it's good to leave something behind, for people to remember you by.

236 It's good to check if your mail-outs arrived. But don't be too full on and give people time to reply.

237 Be nice to people, be respectful.

238 Good work comes through play.

239 Remember you design for the world out there, away from your computer. It's good to step out and enjoy this life.

240 Often people hire you as much for your personality as for your portfolio.

hi

Nederland

241 DESIGN IS A PROCESS. Bad design can kill good management.

242 HONOR THE PAST. There's a lot to learn from our predecessors about drawing, wriling, printing, and thinking. To know the rules is to know how to break them.

243 INITIATE SIDE PROJECTS. Do this for research and development purposes of everything you always wanted to do and learn.

244 DON'T OVERSIMPLIFY. Form is content. Form is added value.

Uitnodiging *Innovatie Anders*
Netwerkbijeenkomst
Health 2.0 in de praktijk

25 feb 09

245
LANGUAGE AS A DESIGN CONCEPT. Language is at the base of communication. Images are at the base of understanding complexity. Combine the best of both worlds and turn design into a visual language.

MORGEN IS HET

di
/ 12
/ 05

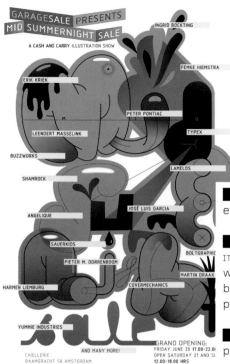

ijsfontein **f**

246 TYPE AS IMAGE. A typeface exists of characters. Build character!

247 THE JOB IS AS FUN AS YOU MAKE IT. Fun is a key factor for quality of work and life. It may take a while before people push the right buttons, push the buttons yourself.

248 Work hard and be nice to people, as a wise man once said.

249 No more Helvetica. Please!

250 Laugh a lot!

Enchilada

www.enchilada.nl

On the 1st of April 2008 Enchilada saw the light of day. One strategist, three designers, and a shared ambition to combine strategic communication with visual power. All four partners have at least ten years of experience each, in Dutch and international design studios. After having run their own companies for several years they found that they share a similar taste for beer and business. They set out to add pepper to visual communication, thus the name *Enchilada* (*enchilar*, Spanish: to add chili pepper). They analyze the position of a client and set strategic goals, make distinct decisions about positioning, and then add value (and chili) through visual concepts. A studio passionate for typography, illustration, and the mechanics of communication, unleashed in their work, in workshops and the side projects: ToyType.com and Sauerkids.com.

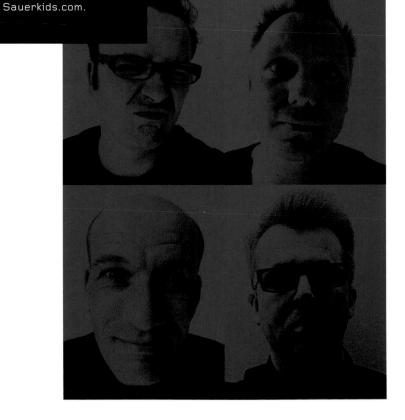

Filip Kleremark

www.kleremark.com

Based in Stockholm, Filip is very passionate about work and has a hunger for problems that need creative solving. His interests lay in digital media and in the way we interact with things in our daily life. With his design, he aims to create solutions for brands that engage, brands that also believe in a better future, brands that believe commercial success can be gained through creativity. A natural raconteur, he enjoys telling stories people want to hear and giving the audience what they might need, not what they already have or have seen before. People react and interact with good ideas, therefore the framework of his ideas is to create work that stays alive, not campaigns that are hot for just a moment. Filip wants to challenge boundaries and constantly evolve himself and the industry. The ad of the future won't be an ad.

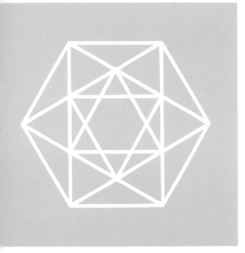

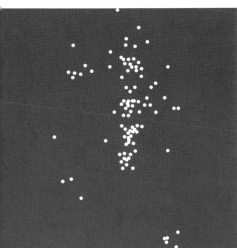

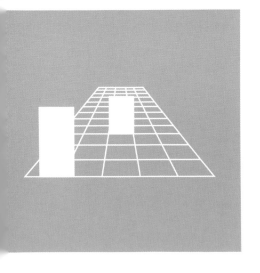

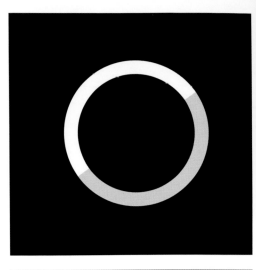

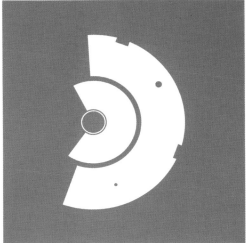

251 ANALYZE THE COMMUNICATIVE PROBLEM. When coming up with an idea I always analyze the communicative problem first and try to find solutions. Research is very important. I stay updated in all different kinds of areas such as fashion, technology, design, etc. I do this through RSS blog feeds, I follow around 300 blogs and spend a lot of time online. I also collect books, packaging, toys, and any other interesting stuff I can find.

252 IDEAS CAN COME FROM ANYWHERE. The creative process is so different depending on the client and their needs. Ideas can really come from anywhere. I don't have a special formula to follow, but it can be useful to change environment sometimes, to get away from the office. I can get an idea while walking on my way home, while sitting in the pub with some friends, or in the middle of the night when I can't sleep.

253 Establish a good relationship between you and the client.

254 Experiment with design and typography.

255
It can be useful to switch environment.

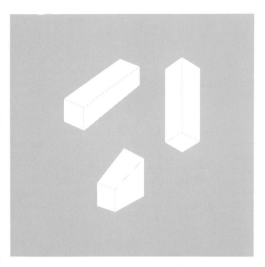

256 ALWAYS ADD A PERSONAL ELEMENT TO YOUR WORK. I integrate my work across all sorts of media. My background is in graphic design but since the industry is changing I have been doing interactive art direction lately. I love Swiss design, and build my foundation on grid systems, but I also experiment with layout, color, and custom typography.

257 A CROWDED MARKET FULL OF VISUAL NOISE. In the case of a project for Rollerboys Recordings the budget was limited so I could only use one color other than black. This was a great challenge. I wanted to do the covers in Pantone colors so that they would look beautiful together as a series with strong typographic treatments following a strict grid. This way the label stands out in a crowded market full of visual noise, releasing records that you want to collect in order to have the complete catalog.

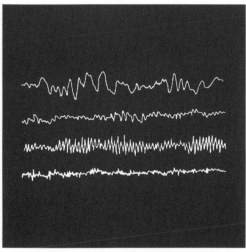

258 FREEDOM IS NICE TO HAVE BUT DIFFICULT TO MANAGE. I have to admit that I'm a bit unorganized. I can sometimes feel that it's hard to start working, I often find myself awake late and then sleep very late the following day. But this is also the case with most of my friends in the creative field. I need structure, the positive side of working for an agency is having definite timetables.

259 AN ONLINE PORTFOLIO IS THE BEST WAY TO PROMOTE WORK. I think that an online portfolio is the best way to promote my work since it's so diverse. It's a lot harder to show motion pieces through a traditional book or a PDF. Make sure design blogs and other influential sites are aware of your website. I feel that a basic site that loads fast and has easy navigation is recommended since people are generally very stressed and need to browse your work quickly.

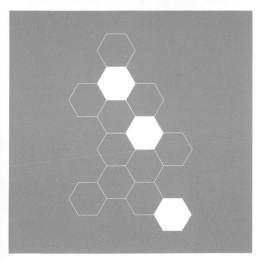

260 Believe in what you do, do what you believe in.

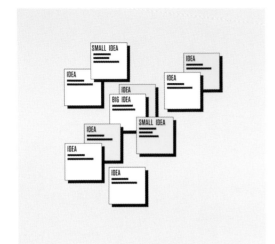

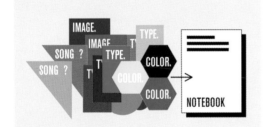

261 One project = one notebook.

262 One idea = one post-it.

263 The same result can be achieved by ways simple or complex, there are no rules.

264 Utilize Internet and the social tools to exchange info (Google reader, graphic design blogs, twitter, etc.). I am an assiduous blog reader. I eat RSS flow!

265 To make choices, to think of several solutions and progressively eliminate all but one, without giving it too much thought.

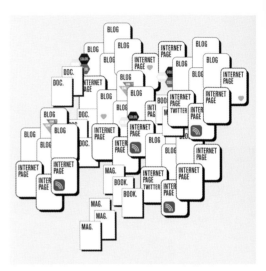

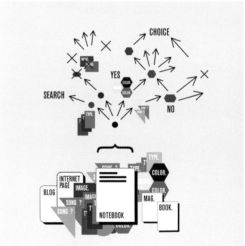

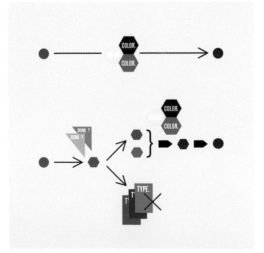

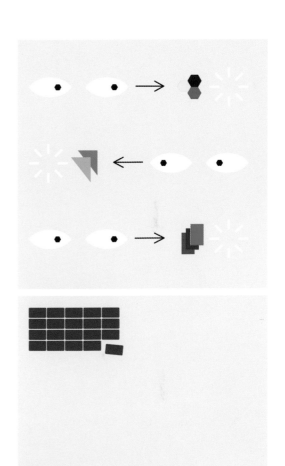

266 Set yourself up for minimum organization; it'll aid to create bases of forms, colors, visual recurrences of favorite subjects, and general graphic elements. Typography is very important, spend time choosing the right one.

267 Don't be afraid of white. Less rather than more.

268 Open eyes and observe— observe and absorb. But learn the limit, and know how to not be too influenced!

269 One chocolate a day keeps bad design away.

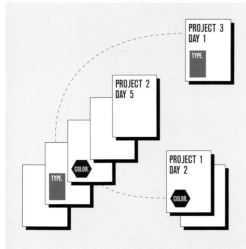

♥ CHOCOLATE.
ONE BY DAY FOR GOOD GRAPHISM.

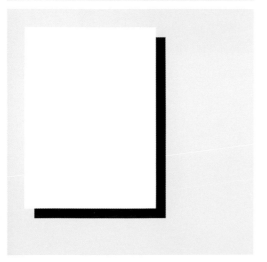

270
Multiply projects and carry them out in parallel. An idea used in a project can also be the solution for another project. So, yes! Ping-Pong!

Florent Guerlain

www.zukunft.fr

Based in the ever trendy Paris, Florent shows an almost mathematical subdivision in interests claiming to have a fascination for politics (25%), food (25%), geometrical forms, statistics and numbers (25%) and others (25%). His work always has a common point: their design is clear and simple, owing to work principally based on typography and forms (he almost never employs photography or 3D elements). Each component used (word, form, special typography, color...) must have an explication. Florent is of the opinion that it is of utmost importance for design to be justified. And if the project can also provoke ideas to the reader, even better. Some of his latest projects include: Hyper!, Crise 2008 (on the current economic crisis), and a graphical identity for Marseille European Cultural Capital 2013.

Forest
www.thisisforest.com

Joel Speasmaker is the founder of Forest, a multi-purpose design studio located in Los Angeles, California, working in the areas of graphic design, art direction, publishing, branding, web design and development, illustration, and various curatorial projects. He previously published *The Drama* magazine, and now acts as art director for *Anthem* magazine, comics section editor for *Swindle* magazine, and conducts interviews for *Faesthetic* magazine. He's been lucky enough to show in galleries such as Subliminal Projects, Little Bird, Lump, Okay Mountain, Thanky, Quirk, and others. He's been featured in books by Victionary, maomao Publications, and Jeremyville, as well as *Flaunt*, *XLR8R*, *Dazed & Confused*, *Entertainment Weekly*, *Art Prostitute*, *Clark*, *Giant Robot*, and *Mule* magazines.

Interaction of Color   **Josef Albers**

Unabridged text and selected plates
Revised edition

271 IDEAS ARE ALREADY INSIDE OF US. It just takes the appropriate project to bring them out and give them shape. Ideas come from our life experiences—through traveling, through interactions with the people we meet, through the books we read, through the music we listen to, through the best and worst of times. There are so many sources of inspiration in even the most seemingly mundane activities.

272 Start with many ideas until you narrow it down to one.

273 AN UNMISSABLE BOOK. *Interaction of Color* by Josef Albers.

274 TRAVEL. Traveling is one of the most important activities to me, not only as a source of ideas but simply as a way to formulate a philosophy of living. All aspects of your life can only benefit by exposure to new and previously unseen and unknown things.

275 YOUR SPACE DEFINES YOUR WORK. Keep your workspace perfectly orderly, surrounded by books and organization.

Recoleta Cemet
enos Aires,
gentina.

Of Great Masses
Moving at Visionary
Speeds.

Things
Volume

We Are Children of
Earth & Sun.

276 Do as many personal projects as possible. Client work will follow.

277 FOLLOW GRIDS (MOST OF THE TIME). Grids are very important, whether you are working for print or web. Even when specifically not following a grid I think it is important to consider its influence in that decision.

278 RESEARCH CONSTANTLY. I am interested and can appreciate most everything I come in contact with, whether it be a work of art, an object, a tool, an idea, a period of history, etc. Because of this, doing specific research for a job is enjoyable.

279 SIMPLE SOLUTIONS. I'm always drawn to the simplest solution, utilizing shape and color to facilitate a meaning for the viewer.

280
If in doubt, print!

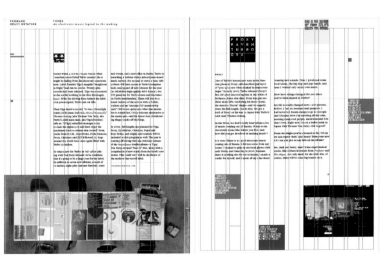

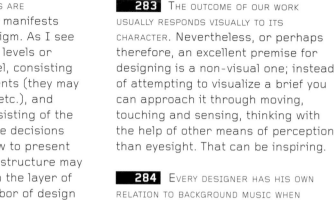

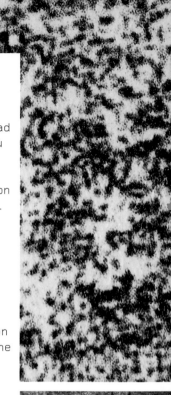

281 IMPORTANT THINGS ARE IMPORTANT. This tautology manifests my dualist design paradigm. As I see it, every design has two levels or dimensions: the top-level, consisting of tangible design elements (they may be images, typography, etc.), and the base structure, consisting of the concept, the thought, the decisions of what to show and how to present that. Although the base structure may be exposed only through the layer of concrete entities, the labor of design should be focused on the invisible. Do not nudge around the elements of your layout; it is inconsequential if an image or typography piece lies here or there. Instead, concentrate on what is important.

282 SKETCH BLOCKS. A friend of mine who is a gifted storyteller once told me a colorful tale of Kaj Franck's sketching habits. The renowned designer used only small cards about 6-inches (15-cm) high for sketching. These so called taco cards were a cheap byproduct of the Tervakoski cardboard factory. The cards were coated on one side and uncoated on the other, making them an excellent platform for both felt pen and pencil drawing. I also use small cards for sketching, and recommend it to everyone.

283 THE OUTCOME OF OUR WORK USUALLY RESPONDS VISUALLY TO ITS CHARACTER. Nevertheless, or perhaps therefore, an excellent premise for designing is a non-visual one; instead of attempting to visualize a brief you can approach it through moving, touching and sensing, thinking with the help of other means of perception than eyesight. That can be inspiring.

284 EVERY DESIGNER HAS HIS OWN RELATION TO BACKGROUND MUSIC WHEN WORKING. When I'm designing I listen to music, but when a project proceeds to production phase, and the work gets a more technical character I often listen to discussion programs with only little music on the radio, or audio books.

285 BRUTALIZE TYPOGRAPHY. Some years ago I visited a lecture by Alex Trüb and Valentin Hindermann where I came across their work for Schauspielhaus Zürich. Their aggressively condensed *Futura* was something that clashed with almost every typographic principle I cherished at the time. This dramatic encounter was the starting shot for the conscious and intentional decay of my typographic taste. Typographic decadence is recommended for anyone!

287   AT THE PRESS. Pen and the Mac are our common tools, and so is the offset press. Therefore at least basic knowledge of the limits and possibilities of the printing process should be a part of every designer's technical expertise. Go to the printer and follow the process whenever possible.

288   LANDSCAPES. I struggled for a long time with a modernist fixation for non-representative layouts. In my opinion, all elements of design should only represent themselves; images should only be images and type especially should never represent anything else but letterforms. I'm now free of this neurotic approach of every layout as a single image, a landscape where everything is possible; type can be as an image, or an image can be typography. Set yourself free!

289   TESTING. Include at least one technical, typographic, or any other sort of test in every project you do. Visiting the area of the unknown makes a design often more challenging to the viewer, and your knowledge expands quickly. Three of four of the tests won't succeed, but who cares? We are not surgeons or pilots, no one dies if you make a mistake, and often no one even notices.

290   Never show the client a sketch you don't want to take further; the client will certainly choose it.

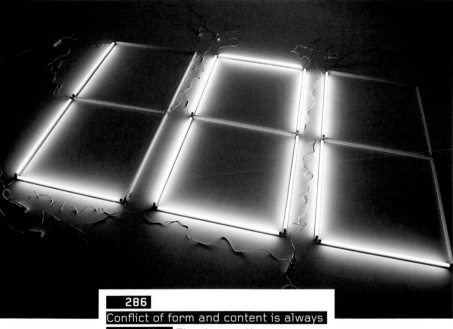

286
Conflict of form and content is always interesting. The deeper the gap between the sublime content and the vulgar form is (or vice versa), the better! When typesetting the Bible, do it with Balloon Extra Bold.

Fräck
www.frck.fi

Jaakko Pietiläinen, the man behind Fräck, founded his agency in 2006. It simultaneously entails an ambition towards a total design concept as well as a passion for detail. Nordic design seems somewhat trendy these days but Jaakko's work continues to reassure us of the absolute solidity of his design. His lines are austere yet playful and his intelligent use of typography reflects formal recognition of the best balance between solid theoretical roots and a passion for experimentation. This style is especially evident in the design and layout of *Tuli&Savu*, a poetry magazine in which the content is adapted to a form that innovates the classic look of that type of publication while contrasting with slightly yellowish stock and a more typewriter style typeface.

Frank Chimero

www.frankchimero.com

An illustrator, graphic designer, and writer in Springfield, Missouri, USA, Frank teaches design and typography at Missouri State Unviersity. He also frequently contributes his writing and illustrations to Thinking for a Living (www.thinkingforaliving. org). He believes in simplicity, honesty, humor, enthusiasm, keeping busy; lots of little things over one big thing. Inspired by the mid-century aesthetic, Frank tries to recapture the sense of optimism, playfulness, heart, and charm that's characteristic of the period. Chimero's fascination with the creative process, curiosity, and visual experience informs all of his work. Each piece is the part of an exploration in finding wit, surprise, honesty and joy in the world around us. For Frank, the work is play, and the play is work.

291 BE HONEST. An open path of communication is built upon trust. Be honest to your audience. This idea is relevant to every other form of communication, and I think it applies to visual communication. Honesty isn't just about audience. Be honest to yourself as well. Do the things you're passionate about. Avoid the things that you hate, if you can.

292 CONSISTENT VOICE IS MORE IMPORTANT THAN CONSISTENT STYLE. Voice is about what you say. It's content. Style is about what you're wearing. It's aesthetics. The prior informs the latter, not the other way around. Clothes don't make the man. They don't make your work either.

293 DOES IT HAVE HEART? If it does, make it. If it doesn't, why spend the time on something that doesn't have spirit?

294 HAVE MODEST EXPECTATIONS. Spend a lot of time choosing that one thing that a piece of design or an illustration should try to do. Then, work your ass off trying to figure out the absolute best way to do that one thing.

295 DON'T BE SCARED OF YOUR TOOLS. Use them, don't fear them. For instance, while sketching, I recommend using cheap paper. If the paper's cheap, you won't feel bad documenting your bad ideas. Getting the first, awful ideas out of the way is crucial: very rarely does any one hit it out of the park on the first try. If I had a sketchbook filled with nice, expensive paper, I'd feel obligated to make the first idea I sketched brilliant. That pressure would paralyze me. Tools should be enablers, not disablers. If something is more intrusive or intimidating than it is useful, get rid of it. It's not a tool, it's a toy. Or worse, a creative boogie man that you're inviting through your front door.

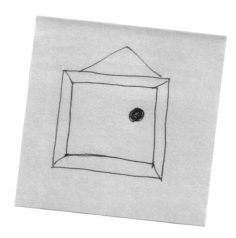

↑ SHARPIE

↑ $14 PEN

296 EXECUTE. An idea on the page is worth 100 times more than an idea in the mind. You can only judge and be judged by work that's executed. Eventually, we all realize that most of the ideas that look great in our mind look dumb once they're real. But, at least you now know.

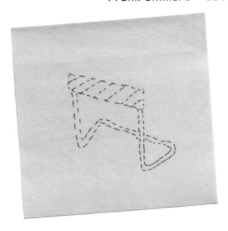

297 EDIT. Delete unimportant things. Even if you love them. If it isn't spectacular, it gets cut. Kill your darlings. Be a cold-blooded killer. Ruthless. Delete. Refine. Improve.

298 BEING TOO COMFORTABLE IS DANGEROUS. Most creatures die in their sleep. Keep moving, or get eaten. The only things you should be absolutely comfortable with in your creative process are your tools.

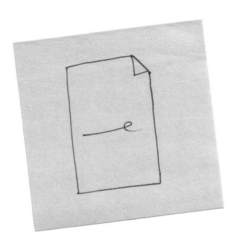

299 THERE IS NOTHING KEEPING YOU FROM DOING THE SORT OF WORK THAT YOU WISH. What do you want? It's a hard, yet crucial question. We all do creative work to get happy. It's why we let it beat us up, and it's why we keep crawling back to it. Figure out precisely what you want, and realize that if no one will pay you to make it, you can still make it for yourself. And you still win, because you're happy.

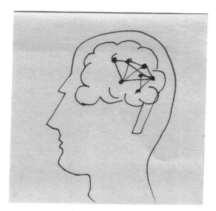

300
Embrace the subconscious. In the studio, I have a sofa for naps with a couple pillows. The pillow is kind of comfortable, but mostly not. Just soft enough to relax you. But, just stiff enough to keep you from falling fully asleep. Right before you fall fully asleep, your brain is making all sorts of connections between all of the unrelated thoughts in your brain. There's no filter from your conscious mind saying: "This makes sense. This other idea doesn't." Without that filter, you can consider more possibilities. So, grab something to write with, fill your head to the brim with research and what you already know. Then, take an almost-nap and get ready to document the ideas that find you.

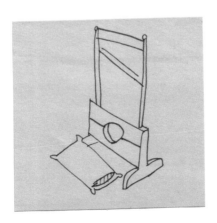

301 THE IDEA IS USUALLY THE TOUGH PART. I believe that for a project to flow most efficiently, the answer has to come very intuitively. So when it doesn't immediately present itself, frustrating times normally follow. When this happens, I generally just start doing miscellaneous research—listening to a podcast like *Radiolab*, reading a book by Malcolm Gladwell or Marty Neuemeier—anything to get me thinking while the project is in the back of my mind. If I'm feeling really lost, I might look back at my older work, or someone else's work to see how I or they have tackled a similar problem, just to gain a perspective. Then after that initial thinking/research, I try to take a break. It's good for me to get up and do something else; maybe I'll go to the store. It eases some of the pressure for me, therefore allowing me to think more clearly and reflect upon that initial thinking.

302 WHEN IDEAS OCCUR, TRY TO EXECUTE THEM RIGHT AWAY ON THE COMPUTER. Other times, I'll scribble down my ideas using words in my sketchbook or on post-it notes. For example, I'm working on an album cover, and here are some notes for a set of concepts I produced. It's a temporary solution, because I certainly can't understand what I wrote a few days later. I have to still be in that same mindset to interpret it.

303 THE IDEAL CLIENT. Description: one who gives you a modest timeline for a good fee, let's you do whatever you wish, and then doesn't complain when you're six months late with the delivery. This, surprisingly, happens, and if it all works out, both parts will be very very happy.

304 TRY TO KEEP A VERY ACTIVE ONLINE LIFE. Whether it's through Twitter, Forums, Blogs, Flickr, Facebook, or whatever. So far, I haven't really placed priority on gaining new projects as much as I have just trying to gain new connections and friends within the design community.

305 LOVE BOOKS. I'm usually so distracted by the pleasant visual design of a book that I have a hard time reading it. My favorite books though, are the ones that get me thinking, motivate me, and usually are about something other than design—but still related to design (like marketing or psychology). Some authors include Malcolm Gladwell, Paul Arden, Jonah Lehrer, and Marty Neuemeier. Also just scavenging around thrift stores for older books with unique, authentic designs tends to yield good inspirational results.

306 WEB PORTFOLIOS. So far, my portfolio has only been presented online. I maintain a website that showcases what I feel is the work that best represents me. I also maintain a Behance site with the same projects. And then I have a Flickr, which I generally use to just throw up new work, whether it was a quick doodle, a serious piece, or even a preview of a new project I'm working on. With clients and prospective clients, I'll usually send them my portfolio website, and my Flickr. I only send those two, because I've heard stories about how some clients hate receiving PDFs, and an easily navigational website is often a better way to communicate your brand than a generic PDF.

FLICKR
BEHANCE
TWITTER
ETC.

WORK

308 PREFER A MORE RELAXED
ENVIRONMENT. I'll put on some music, or
even have a movie/TV show playing in a
corner of the computer monitor. Music
I tend to enjoy is generally something
atmospheric, like Animal Collective, Nice
Nice, Brian Eno, Neu!, or even Igor
Stravinsky.

309 RESEARCH IS ONE OF THE MOST
IMPORTANT ASPECTS OF THE DESIGN PROCESS.
I believe that one should never stop
researching during a project. In order
for me to begin the research, my brain
has to be working properly, so I'll have
some coffee or tea, and put on a podcast
which will help me to start thinking. Then
I'll do some visual research, by either
looking through my archive folder of
saved images or looking on Ffffound or
through my bookmarks to see if anything
inspires me. I'll think of keywords and
search through Wikipedia, on Flickr, or
Google Images to see what comes up,
and often find myself on many random
tangents. I'll look through my selection
of books, I'll write notes, etc. I try to
immerse myself with a ton of related and
unrelated imagery and information to
how I perceive the project.

310 DOING LITTLE EXPERIMENTS WILL
GREATLY INFORM YOUR WORK. There are
two things that have stuck with me
throughout my career as a designer.
One is a quote by Paul Arden which
states: "Experience is the opposite of
creativity." Whenever I'm stuck on a
project, I think of this and realize that
anything is possible. You don't have to
have a big name in design to be able
to accomplish what you wish—you just
have to do it, and you can do it however
you wish. Intuition is an important asset
to creativity, and you should value it. The
other thing is something I came upon
when researching for a project in my
first year in design school. It was how
Stefan Sagmeister sometimes generates
ideas, and he has three processes
that he recommends. One is a timed
outcome, whatever you can generate in
a few hours. Second is picking a random
card from a deck of Brian Eno's *Oblique
Strategy* card set. And third is picking
a random word from a dictionary and
starting from there. To me, it's not the
process of these recommendations
that are important, but it's the idea of
doing something random to generate
a random idea. I believe that exploring
new experiences, techniques, cultures,
mediums, and collaborations is a great
way of bringing a fresh approach to
your work.

307
BUSY VS. NON-BUSY. If I'm busy and
in the "zone," my workspace will be
horribly chaotic with books, notes,
pencils, pens, paintbrushes, drinking
glasses, bowls, papers, etc. Even my
cat likes to get involved in the chaos.
If I'm not working on anything, I
prefer it to be clean.

Gavin Potenza

www.gavinpotenza.com

A communicative designer living in Portland, Oregon, he enjoys thought-provoking design that is both unexpected and inspiring. He strives to do many things in his life. Currently freelances full-time and also participates in outside creative ventures such as a collaborative partnership known as Joug, where the two explore various activities such as art shows, publication design, and album package artwork. As well, he enjoys working on projects, and thinking about projects. On occasion, Gavin Potenza will author posts in different graphic design blogs. Latest projects include: I am Mercedes— where he directed artistically and designed the look of the core navigation to a website that visualizes data from a survey uf Mercedes drivers in the UK.

Goodmorning Technology

www.gmtn.dk

Goodmorning Technology is a strategic design firm that enables companies to strengthen their brand and achieve business success through design, communication, and innovation. They create the worlds in which the clients' products, services, and identities exist, helping clients use design and innovation as a business parameter. Goodmorning Technology is of the conviction that design is the way for a strong product development and effective communication. By means of genuine love for design the company uses their "magenta power" to push innovation forward, to investigate and to dare, to get out of the box, and to do things others haven't done yet. This enables clients to achieve their strategic goals through a broad range of creative tools, each used to its best effect. Their motto: "Relax, it will be perfect!"

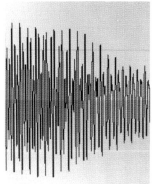

311 THE IDEA IS KING. An idea is a result of something; if nothing is put into the equation nothing will come out. Get up, go out, surf the web, explore, photograph, absorb, listen to music, go to the theater, and check out art and all other kinds of visual stimuli. Great design for us is great ideas. The idea is key. It is easy to make good looking design, but without a great idea behind it the design won't stand out in the long run. Go into depth with the range of products you are working on, both your client and the competition, find that little detail that makes your product special and can eventually make your design the best.

312 DOODLE! Sketchbooks and notepads or the back of an envelope—paper is definitely a good place to start. It's easy to go directly to the computer, but often it pays to sketch and doodle your way through your initial ideas. This way you can play and explore different options. At this stage it is about finding the right idea, not about creating pretty visuals.

313 THINK FONTS. Handle with care; don't use theme fonts, don't use Brush Script, but don't hate either, use Times if it works, use Helvetica or Akkurat, use Akzidenz (maybe the new one), use Avenir, Avenir Next, ITC Avant Garde, maybe even Futura, Klavika, Garamond, Didot, Utopia, Trade Gothic, News and Letter Gothic. Go bold, go thin, draw your own logotypes and maybe a whole font, but read and study hard. There are a lot of rules—some are to be followed some are to be broken. Use simple colors, or keep the type in black and white. Select the sizes carefully and make test prints, do not trust your screen. Try setting the font in higher points than you know would work, and lower. By seeing a completely wrong size it is easier to pinpoint the right one. Do not use fonts that are too similar, try to achieve contrast in your designs and have fun!

314 TRY SOMETHING NEW. When choosing colors for your project, be conscious of the effect of the colors. Do I want a sleek looking design? Luxurious? Cheap? Fun? Serious? Do I want my design to scream or to whisper? Either way, use colors with care and take your time choosing them. Use new, odd colors and combine them in new ways to achieve a design that might take getting used to but stands out. In the end it just might result in a unique look for your client.

315 USE GRIDS AND RULES WHEN DESIGNING. Grids are what you build design on. Unfortunately far too much design now is done without grids. That said, not everything has to be done with grids but exceptions should be deliberate. Look at design from fifty years ago, designers from those days knew what to align to the grid and when and how to break away from it. So use grids and keep on developing them for innovative and quality designs.

317 BE YOURSELF. Often you catch yourself being overly concerned with what the client wants and expects from you and your work(place). If all is well, the client is there to meet you and your workplace at it is, so don't fuss over being overly perfect and overly dressed. If you dress in a certain way it is probably a mirror of your abilities as a designer, so keep it that way. And your clients will respect you and your work as a complete package.

318 CHOOSE THE RIGHT CLIENTS. The ideal client is hard to find, and hard to envision. When looking for new clients it is often not the most interesting companies that are the most interesting clients. Often these have already found their way of communicating with design. The most interesting clients are therefore the ones you can help and move onto the right path. They might need a bit of convincing but if they are open for change then this is where you can really make some giant steps towards a better product.

319 DON'T BE A SLAVE OF YOUR TOOLS. We love our digital tablets, pens are so much more natural than the normal mouse. It's about making designs that are not defined by your tools. So the consumers are not thinking of how the design was made but simply how it looks and what it means to them!

320 DON'T BE JUST A DESIGNER! Step out of the designing role once in a while: act as a consumer, act as an older person or someone younger. What could make this project outstanding? Ask around: ask your mother and her mother; ask your nerdy friend and your worst enemy! Ask yourself questions about the complete project: Should the product/service/company itself be changed somehow? Is the name right? Does it play up to the design, or are they fighting against each other? Could we come up with a campaign for the product instead of a new pack, is the tone of voice right? Challenging the overall project on all levels makes the entire project better and creates the best platform for a unique design.

316
PROMOTE YOUR PROJECT AS IF IT WAS THE BEST PROJECT EVER MADE. Never doubt your project; if you do, others will too. Use your website, blogs, books to promote your work. The Internet has not lost its power of impact. A video of the Widex box (one of our studio's best projects) in action was put on YouTube for fun and promotion. Quickly it spread across design blogs all over the world and YouTube chose the video as pick of the day. This resulted in more than 60,000 views of the video (probably double this when all the blogs are counted). The promotion has also brought international clients to our studio that would never have found us otherwise.

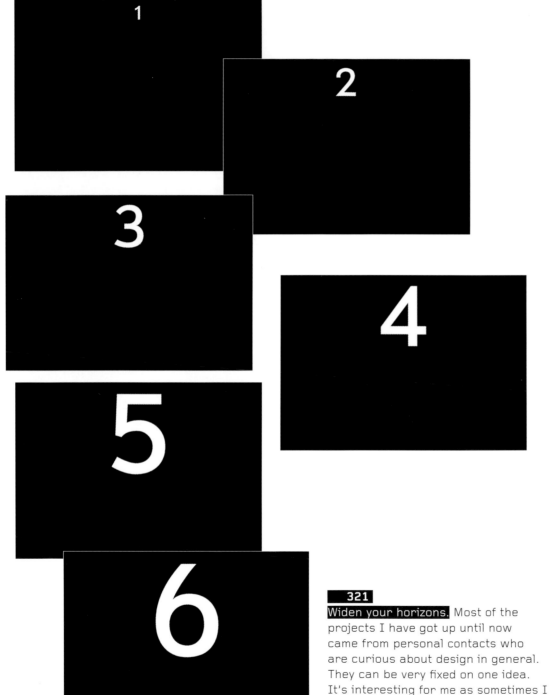

322 START RIGHT AWAY. While I am talking with the client for the first time I'm already thinking. But ideas often come while I am doing something else.

323 BOOKS ARE IMPORTANT. Every book can be recommended. It is good to be critic and to look at the mistakes and/or positive aspects of each one.

324 CLEANER DESKTOPS. The work space should not contain too many things.

325 STAGE PRESENCE. I prefer to be serious and friendly at the same time. They like each other.

326 Keep it simple.

321
Widen your horizons. Most of the projects I have got up until now came from personal contacts who are curious about design in general. They can be very fixed on one idea. It's interesting for me as sometimes I have to convince them to opt for other design solutions.

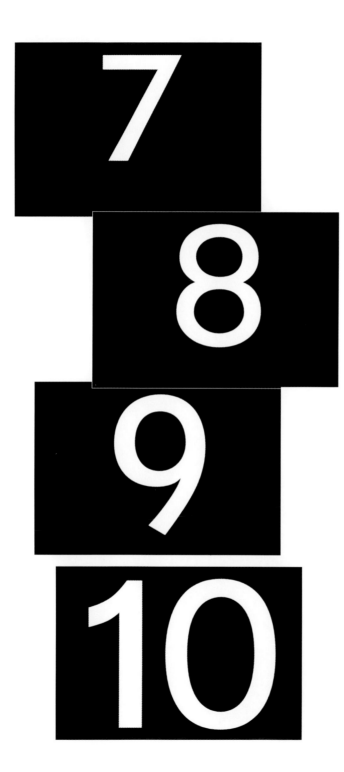

327 STICK TO GRIDS. Grids are nice and help us to structure our ideas. But don't abuse it!

328 BE A REGULAR AT THE PRINT SHOP. I have the chance to work with a great and very small print workshop in Zurich: René Wüest, Printservice.

329 FOLLOW YOUR PROJECT. Following the project from A to Z is very important for me. What you see on your computer will never exactly look like the printed result.

330 PROMOTE YOURSELF. I use the website sortby.org to show self-initiated work. Designers on sort by have the possibility to have their own page with a short biography and an address to be contacted by people who are interested in their work.

Guillaume Mojon

www.sortby.org/person/GuillaumeMojon

A Swiss designer who lives and works in Zurich. After working for various graphic design studios in Berlin and in Switzerland he completed a Master of Arts program at the Werkplaats Typografie in Arnhem, the Netherlands. His work is often self-initiated and focuses mainly on typography. Together with Francesca Grassi, he conceived sortby. org, a website/platform showing a selection of autonomous and self-initiated work by designers. One of his most featured projects was *Biography of Lawrence Weiner*, where Guillaume transferred statements of Lawrence Weiner into type installations. Using the spaces of his workshop to build everything with boxes, tape, spray, and other kinds of found material. In this way he represented the meaning of Weiner's separate works. The spacial translations were then documented in a series of five photographs.

Hansje van Halem
www.hansje.net

Hansje van Halem graduated as a graphic designer from the Gerrit Rietveld Academie, Amsterdam in 2003 and has been working as an independent graphic designer since. Besides designing books and invitations for several cultural institutes in the Netherlands,

Hansje loves to draw type—which she sometimes incorporates in commissioned designs. The biggest exposure came in 2007 when Hansje designed two postage stamps, which have been filling people's mailboxes for the past two years. She teaches for workshops in different art schools

in the Netherlands as well as abroad. Her work forms part of the Stedelijk Museum and Van Abbemuseum's collections. Latest projects include an invitation for an exhibit at Hotel Mariakapel, a publication for an exhibition in the MMKA, Arnhem.

331 Find a base, something to hold on to.

332 Work within the given boundaries.

333 Don't repeat, just think.

334 Create new boundaries.

335 Interpret new boundaries.

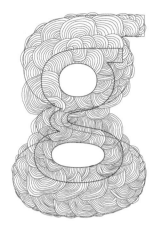

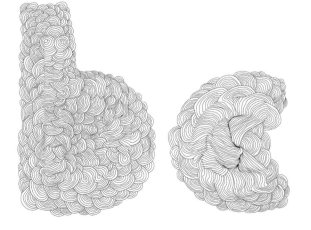

336 Don't think, keep repeating.

337 Take a look, fill the gaps.

338 Take a look and judge.

339 Don't mind errors, save them.

340 Don't mind irregularities, save them.

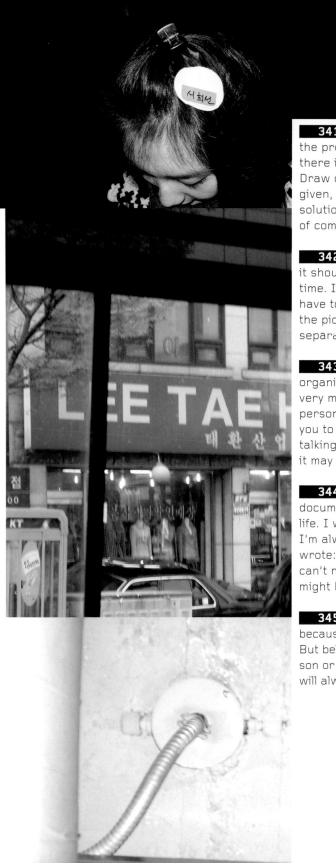

341 Easy but essential: find the problem. If there is no problem, there isn't going to be an answer. Draw out every possible problem given, and turn them all into creative solutions. I have this very bad habit of complaining about life in Korea.

342 Deviate from the custom, but it should be acceptable at the same time. I ask myself, why do name cards have to have 8 pt letters, or why do the pictures in a book have to be separated from the text, etc.

343 Chaos on the outside, yet organized on the inside. My place is very messy, but I'm a very organized person. It is a fact that mess leads you to creativity. And I'm not only talking about it in the work place, but it may be applied to design itself.

344 Have the very desire to document everything that happens in life. I write a personal journal, and I'm always carrying a camera. I even wrote: "I dreamt about something I can't remember." Someday all of this might be very useful, who knows...

345 Present yourself to the world, because they won't be coming to you. But believe that *you* are the god, or the son or the daughter of a god, and you will always have good luck.

347 Don't ever feel the pressure that you have to create something new all the time. Whatever you do exists, or existed at some point in history, somewhere in this world. Relieved? But, at the same time, do wonder: "Is there really nothing left to say?"

348 This is the philosophy of my life. If you are given two options of doing it or not doing it, don't ever hesitate. I've learned in my life experience that doing it is always best. Haven't thought about it in design though...

349 A design is nothing without your thought, or philosophy. The just-look-good designs get a hundred, a thousand, a million, a trillion times better with a bit of your idea, yourself.

350 All of these thousand tips are useless unless you drink, smoke, dance, make love, and have fun. Enjoy everyone!

346
50% is luck, 30% is skill, and 20% is personal network. If you think you are unlucky, and your design sucks, go out and make lots of friends.

Heesun Seo

www.hxx.kr

A young designer originally from Korea, Heesun studied at Kookmin University, South Korea. She was born in Seoul but she started globetrotting at an early age and lived in Costa Rica, Colombia, and Brazil. All in all she has lived in thirteen different places and studied in eight different schools and her multicultural life experience is evident in her work. Her interests lie in vintage, elegant, chaotic, and minimal design all at the same time. One of her most prominent projects is UIT design & law, in collaboration with Bora Kim. The booklet is about a very interesting combination of two different fields, design and law. While having a serious look and being very neatly organized, it's also enriched with design details in the margins, photos, and strokes.

Hello

www.01134.co.uk

After being founded in 2001, the agency decided for a radical change of location to a farm in rural Somerset, wanting a relaxed and inspirational environment in which to work. As it shows in their work, they couldn't be happier. Hello designs because of love. Each new brief is a challenge and the opportunity gives them a way to explore new means of communicating. The agency strives to work with an open mind. Some of the best solutions can be found in the most unexpected of places, so it's common practice not to stick rigidly to one house style or process. The process is simple: make some coffee (or green tea), open the studio doors onto the sunny Somerset countryside, and chuck plenty of ideas about. Ethic is equally uncomplicated: meeting clients' needs and exceed their expectations.

in**dependent**

web log

351 Remain small. It allows you to retain your integrity and independence as a designer and not be dependent on your clients.

352 Work with nice clients, sack nasty ones—nasty clients create stress, unhappy people, and sleepless nights.

353 Love grids.

354 Keep a blog of your work in progress and things you like. Also read other people's blogs regularly. They are more instant than design books as a resource, and as they are constantly updated—feeding your appetite for inspiration.

no sleep

"hero"

355 Go to lectures. It's easy to forget how truly inspiring these talks can be, and it's also easy to forget why some of the greats are the greats. Remind yourself of what can be achieved.

keming.

m··i··n··d

356 Take on projects that are outside your comfort zone, and approach them with an open mind, the lack of experience will produce interesting results.

357 Pay attention to detail— dashes, kerning, numbers, spacing, etc. Small, but hugely important.

358 Don't present stuff that you don't believe in—clients will inevitably pick it, and you will have to live a lie for the remainder of the project.

359 Research (and not just in Google).

360 Love Helvetica.

research

believe

love.hate

361 Listen,

362 look,

363 think,

364 plan,

365 sort,

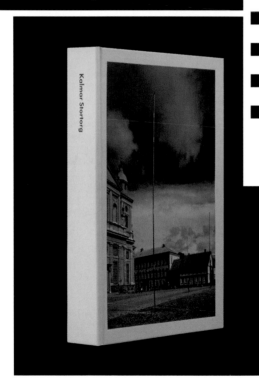

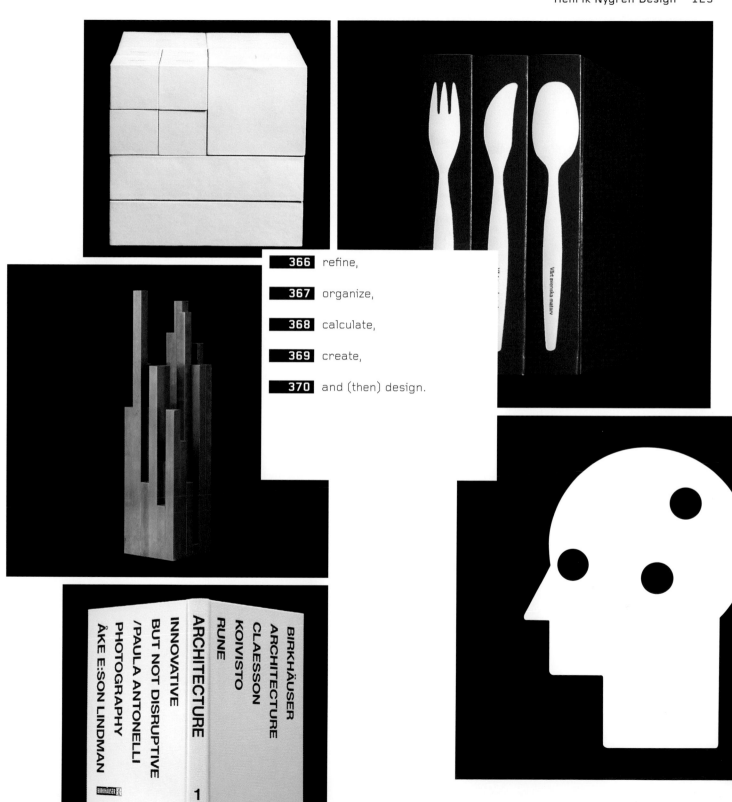

366 refine,

367 organize,

368 calculate,

369 create,

370 and (then) design.

Henrik Nygren Design

www.henriknygrendesign.se

An accomplished Swedish designer, he has received dedicated exhibitions in Tokyo, Malmö, and Stockholm. Recipient of the 2007 Platinum Egg and Berling Award. He has been well represented throughout the years at the Guldägget, Form, Svensk Bokkonst, and Art Directors Club of Europe awards. Henrik Nygren Design mainly works analyzing the client's market potential, developing a strategy in accordance with this potential and the design and production of books, magazines, packaging, corporate identities, advertising campaigns, exhibitions. When necessary, and depending on the nature of the assignment, the company enlists a carefully selected group of brand strategists, copywriters, and printers. Clients choose the agency to obtain the greatest possible quality from given circumstances.

Hey

www.heystudio.es

Tilman Solé and Verónica Fuerte form Hey, a multi-disciplinary design studio specializing in brand management, editorial design, packaging, and interactive media. Tilman specialized in industrial design at *Toni Arola Studio* and *Rosa Lázaro*. Verónica studied Graphic Gesign at Elisava, and went on to specialize in typography at Eina, Escola d'Art i Disseny. They share the conviction that good design means combining content, functionality, graphic expression, and strategy. Both know that ideas are important, but the transition to reality is key. Design is all about transforming good ideas into successful and adequate graphic solutions for each project. They are passionate about their job in every detail. Clients include: Generalitat de Catalunya, Intermón Oxfam, Edicions 62, Empúries, *W*, Trivial Music, Summa, and Barlesa.

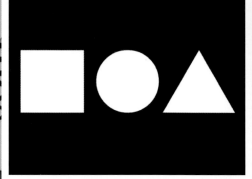

371 REFER TO THE PAST. Design re-invents itself. Be aware of the past in contemporary design.

372 IDEAS. Getting good ideas is the foundation for any project.

373 IDEAS SHOULD BE EASY TO UNDERSTAND. Less is more. Try to compress an idea to the maximum.

374 CLIENT RELATIONS. Have a positive attitude, a custom way of thinking design. Fresh and friendly client service.

375 PRODUCTION. Always think about color combinations when designing identities.

376 CREATE/EXPERIMENT. Make time to experiment with design.

377 PROMOTION. Promoting oneself is very important and it goes more digital everyday. It seems that today's alternative communication is paper. It transmits things that are impossible to convey through a screen.

378 TYPOGRAPHY. We don't have a favorite font, trying out what works best in the correct context, and customizing fonts is important.

379 BE UPDATED. Be informed on everything that's going on in the world, not only in graphic design. Cinema, architecture, photography, and more.

380 FOLLOW A BEACON. Paul Rand is a major source of inspiration.

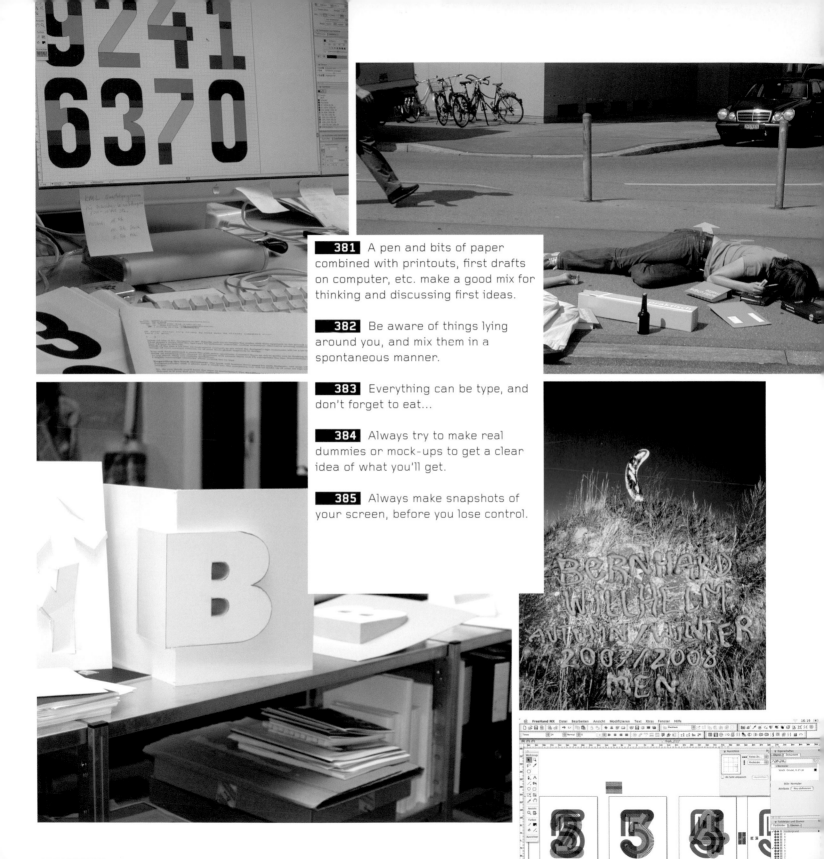

381 A pen and bits of paper combined with printouts, first drafts on computer, etc. make a good mix for thinking and discussing first ideas.

382 Be aware of things lying around you, and mix them in a spontaneous manner.

383 Everything can be type, and don't forget to eat…

384 Always try to make real dummies or mock-ups to get a clear idea of what you'll get.

385 Always make snapshots of your screen, before you lose control.

BERNHARD WILHELM
AUTUMN/WINTER
2007/2008
MEN

386 Listen to some really nice music that'll keep you going. For example: www.stadtfilter.ch.

387 Spend your holidays with good friends, take an inspiring project idea to be developed with you, and start thinking while doing something else.

388 Create a cool website and hope that it will be posted on design blogs. That's the best promotion you'll get.

389 Work on current projects as well as you can. Old jobs create new ones.

390 THE BIGGER THE TYPE, THE BETTER THE POSTER.

Hi

www.hi-web.ch

Megi Zumstein and Claudio Barandun founded Hi in January 2007. Megi studied Visual Communication at the Zürcher Hochschule der Künste (Zurich School of Art and Design). Her diploma work *Visualization of Language* has been awarded with different prizes and has been featured in exhibitions in Zurich, Sarnen, Paris, Tehran, and Ingolstadt. She teaches Graphic Design at the Hochschule Luzerne, where Claudio Barandun got his degree in Design. Their clients include Universities of Applied Sciences of central Switzerland and different small private companies. Some of Claudio's posters have been awarded at 100 Best Posters in Germany, Austria, and Switzerland, the ADC Prize Switzerland and the Poster Biennial in Tehran. He is co-editor of the magazine *Strapazin* (www.strapazin.ch).

Hype Type Studio
www.hypetype.co.uk

Formed in 1999 by Paul Hutchison, Hype Type Studio is a multi-disciplinary graphic design and communications agency with over ten years experience working closely with local, national, and international clients. The firm has built a reputation for producing relevant, memorable, and effective creative solutions. Although already well established, Hype Type Studio has decided to avoid specialization and keeps a wide range of clients, so they can keep creating a wide range of projects. Their extensive array ranges from sleek editorial and packaging designs for corporate clients to global identity and logo creation. Nevertheless, the smaller more independent projects retain the same cutting-edge style and quality whether t-shirt design, illustration, or websites.

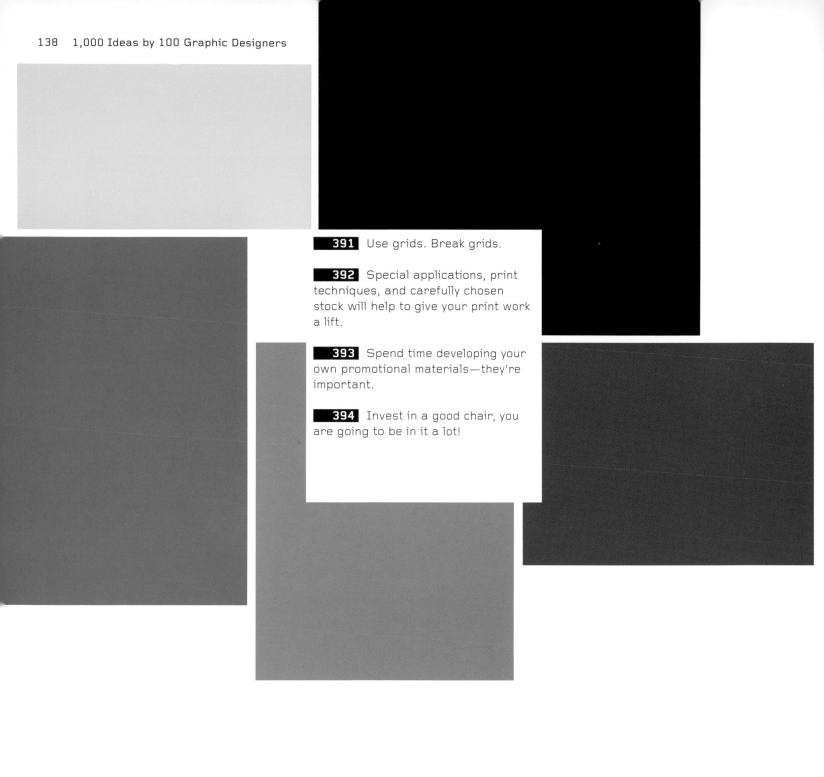

391 Use grids. Break grids.

392 Special applications, print techniques, and carefully chosen stock will help to give your print work a lift.

393 Spend time developing your own promotional materials—they're important.

394 Invest in a good chair, you are going to be in it a lot!

395 Choose your suppliers carefully. Outstanding quality and service is essential.

396 Give your consultancy and encourage feedback. Work in collaboration with your clients.

397 Present your concepts well. Back up your ideas by discussing your thought process. Explain why your chosen direction works.

398 When starting a project, draft your ideas using a method you are most comfortable with—sketch, digital, etc.

399 Enjoy what you do.

400
Don't let your clients' budget restrict your creativity.

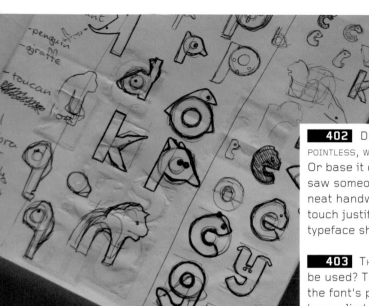

402 DESIGNER TYPEFACES ARE OFTEN POINTLESS, WHY NOT GIVE IT A PURPOSE? Or base it off of something? I once saw someone design a font around neat handwriting. This personal touch justified it. Whatever it is, your typeface should have a reason to exist.

403 THINK OF PLACE. Where will it be used? Think long and hard about the font's purpose and where it will be applied. Is it a header font or is it for body text? If it is for both then you may need to think about different weights.

404 LOOK AT EXAMPLES. Take notes on what makes a typeface work, or what gives it a specific tone. Also make sure that what you're aiming for has not been done a million times over. There is nothing wrong with wanting to put your own stamp alongside others, but you may find it difficult to best them. Also you'll get more recognition for something unique.

405 REMEMBER, UNIQUE AND OBSCURE ARE VERY DIFFERENT THINGS. Try and base it either off of something meaningful to you or give it a purpose in the real world. Designing a typeface out of nothing but semi-circles is falling back into pointless territory.

401

DESIGN A FONT. IT'S HARD BUT WORTH IT. Creating a font takes a lot of time and effort, not because it is hard to use typeface software, but because of the amount of tweaking involved. Anyone with an experience of working in illustrator can produce a typeface, and it's an impressive thing to include in your portfolio.

Never been feature
tell me about his
Billy Blue Colleg

Posted in Graduate

Jamie Grego
January 5th, 2009

406 WHEN WORKING ON A FONT, SAVE A NEW FILE EVERYDAY AND NAME IT BY DATE. It is nice to show the development of one project in your portfolio—make that project your typeface. Seeing the evolution of your font's characters communicates itself and displays the effort that you have put in.

407 MAKE SURE THAT YOU DISPLAY YOUR FONT AS IT IS INTENDED TO BE USED. Only laying out the characters may look pretty, but it says nothing for the font's spacing or whether it is successful in its application.

408 EXPAND. If your font has been designed with a specific application in mind, now think about expanding on this. Within reason could it break into any other mediums? How would it look on staff t-shirts for example?

409 RESTRAIN YOURSELF. List all of your ideas on how the font can be used and then pick one or two great examples. Do not pick more than this for the sake of adding easy work to your portfolio. There is a fine line between having an ambitious project and milking the same idea. People will notice when you are milking it and will grow tired of it very quickly.

410 SUBMIT YOUR WORK TO DESIGN BLOGS. They are a great way to get publicity and to make your font known. While it's a given that any design work can be submitted to a blog, I think fonts are much better received because all designers need them.

abcdefghi
jklmnopqr
stuvwxyz

v1.1 rdefghi
    ınopqr
stuvwxyz

Jamie Gregory

www.thisdesignismine.co.uk

Jamie Gregory is a London-based graphic designer currently carrying out freelance work. He studied BA (Honors) Graphic Design at Central Saint Martins College of Art and Design and graduated with an upper second-class degree (2.1). His talent for design started to emerge during his second year studies when he was awarded a D&AD commendation for his entry to the global student awards. Jamie works in print-based design including books, editorial, posters, stationery, corporate identity, signage, and typeface design, and has a love for design that serves a specific purpose. One of his latest projects is the Zoological typeface—an expansion of the typeface VAG Rounded developed specifically for zoo signage. The project also included design of maps and staff uniforms.

Janine Rewell

www.janinerewell.com

A freelance graphic designer and illustrator from Helsinki. Her awarded work has appeared in advertisements, product packaging, book covers, magazines, and posters. Janine's computer-based vector style combines basic geometrical forms with small decorative elements. The style is often described as absurd yet naive, with a modern Slavic touch. Janine has studied Graphic Design and Illustration at Taideteollinen korkeakoulu (University of Art and Design Helsinki) and Rhode Island School of Design (RISD, 2008). As an illustrator she is represented by the Finnish illustration agency Agent Pekka. She was recently awarded with silver in the illustration category, Best of The Year 2008 (Kuva ja Kuvitus, Vuoden Huiput) Grafia, Finland.

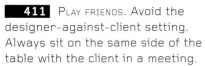

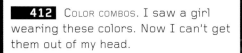

411 PLAY FRIENDS. Avoid the designer-against-client setting. Always sit on the same side of the table with the client in a meeting.

412 COLOR COMBOS. I saw a girl wearing these colors. Now I can't get them out of my head.

413 LIBRARY OF INSPIRATION. Create a library on your computer with subfolders for different categories like "type," "posters," etc. Follow design blogs daily. Every time you see something cool take a screenshot and save it in the library. When you face a problem, browse through these files to get inspired. This is much faster than bookmarks.

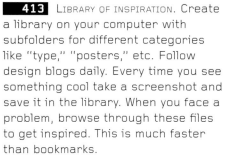

414 CLIENTS AND CLOTHES. When you go to a business meeting, wear your best underwear. Self-confidence comes from beneath.

415 SKETCHBOOKS. I wasn't accustomed to sketch. Nowadays I can't manage without it. Sketches are especially handy when it comes to long projects during which you tend to forget where it all started from.

416 DEADLINES. I organize my working schedules with post-it notes. Different colors for different tasks. I have the notes above my desk so that I can't simply miss them.

417 HABITS. I have a weakness for die cuts. I don't know why. What's yours?

418 THINKING SPOT. Try not to stare at your screen 24/7. Usually my best ideas come when I move my eyes from virtual windows to real ones.

419 WEBSITE. Your website is what you are. Don't leave your portfolio in the middle of a messy code.

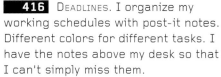

TIME

420 SHORTCUTS. BY LEARNING ALL THE SHORTCUTS YOU'LL SAVE HUNDREDS OF WORKING HOURS. LEARN ONE EVERY DAY UNTIL YOU CAN USE THEM ALL.

en a designer, his work and design process.

NINE
RE/
WELL

Graphic Design
   Tuli & Savu
   Packaging music
   Christmas Greetings
   Mandala
   Smiles for miles
   Escape Diary
   Nolla magazine
   Geopool
   Relative directions
   Spork package
   Font
   Attention book
   Price of Beauty
Illustration
About
Contact

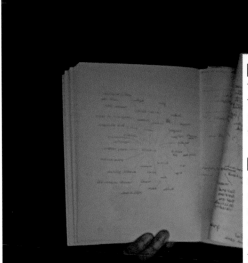

421 MIND MAPS. When I start coming up with ideas I take time creating mind maps, putting into words and diagrams what's going on in my brain. The messier the map, the clearer my thoughts after.

422 MUSIC. When I need to concentrate and stay focused, I listen to instrumental music with repetitive themes. I'll listen to those tracks or entire albums over and over again while I work. This helps me focus and sets me in a time that is continuous, that seems to pause, slow down, and last forever. It shuts me out of the world around me and sits me comfortably in a space that's mine.

423 TIMES NEW ROMAN. It's one of my favorite fonts. It's a font you can find everywhere. Everyone has it. It works on the Internet. No problem converting it. It's a classic font you can do a lot with. While it may feel very standard to many, it is not to me when used in new curious ways.

424 PAPER. Choosing the right paper for your project is important. Order samples. Verify how your artwork prints: how do the colors work on it? Will the colors lose brightness? Will the black streak? Will the text bleed? Will it show on the other side? Also make sure the weight of the paper is right: does it give you the lightness intended? or the thickness desired? Once you finally have made your mind up, don't forget to pay attention to the direction of the grain when you order it!

425 IDEAS. When I begin searching for ideas around a theme, I use Google Images, dictionaries, books, manuals, flyers, posters, friends, movies, and signage as inspiration. I'm on constant look-out for ideas.

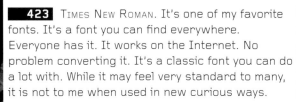

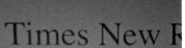

Times New R

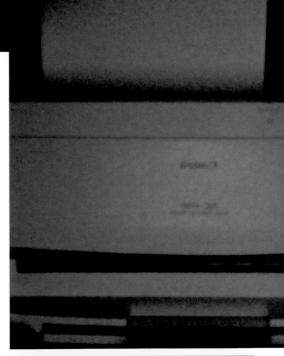

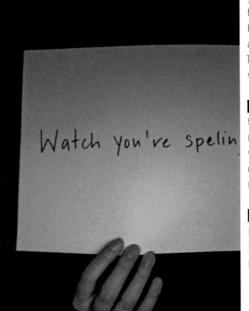

426 DESIGNING IS LIKE INVESTIGATING. When I first start a project and learn about the theme, I read a lot, try to understand what I am working on, what the content is about. And with what I have learnt, I use as much as I can in my graphic solutions. This way my design is as closely linked to my content, in as many fresh new ways as possible.

427 SPELLING. There is an add-on tool named Pro Lexis used with InDesign. It enables you to correct your spelling, grammar and typographic spaces, punctuation, and more. It helps you make something as close to perfection as possible. Spelling and punctuation mistakes look terrible in books. Just why it isn't included with InDesign is yet a mystery to me.

428 RESTRICT YOURSELF WITH LIMITATIONS. Base the choice of your limitations on rational and meaningful decisions. You could go black and white for cost reasons, you could use only a certain type size for legibility reasons if you are making a book for the nearly blind, for example.

429 PRINT. Throughout your project, print, print, print. Check what you're doing by printing bits of your work as you go. Some things look good on screen but not necessarily on paper.

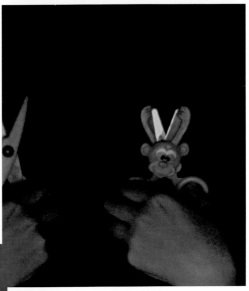

430 COMMON PEOPLE. I'm interested and inspired by all tools that people who aren't familiar with graphic design use. Try to design using Word, Photobooth, and Acrobat Reader.

Jessica Scheurer

www.kaysl.ch

Jessica Scheurer was born in Miami in 1985, but grew up happily by the lake in the beautiful land of clockworks and chocolates (Switzerland). Having always loved paper and pens, she readily studied at ECAL (Ecole Cantonale d'Art de Lausanne). In summer of 2008 she graduated with a Bachelor degree in Graphic Design and left the school with a bit of extra baggage: her oversized laptop. During the course of her studies she zealously continued to travel as much as in her childhood, practicing her Spanish and German. Her latest projects include: Hai (a typography based on hand-brush painting), Death_talks (a diploma project around death featuring 3 interviews, 2 scientific texts, and 11 tables), and new year invitation cards for Praline studio.

Jihad Lahham

www.jihadlahham.com

After a happy childhood playing in the streets of Damascus, Jihad grew up observing and absorbing thousands of years of accumulated culture. His infatuation with art began when he watched his father copying masterpieces by Van Gogh, Claude Monet, Pierre-Auguste Renoir, and Alfred Sisley.

At the age of eleven his art school submitted one of his pieces for a competition, and to his surprise he was picked as one of the top 200 young artists in the world. His interests in visual communication developed going through freshman year in college. Jihad has won several competitions and honors

including the Trustee Scholarship and the Rockport International Industrial Design student competition for two consecutive years. His work experience includes companies in Syria, Dubai, Saudi Arabia, and the US including J.A.M.P.tv, Yellow Hits, and EA games.

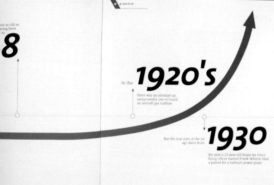

431 LET THE BEAUTY OF THE TYPEFACE SHOW. Don't kill it with too many treatments. Good typefaces have been immaculately developed and designed to look good on their own on a white page, so some minimal treatment might not be a bad idea, but that has to really be minimal, otherwise it would compromise the integrity of the typeface. Keep in mind every case has an exception, but stay faithful to the spirit of the text.

432 SHOW, DON'T TELL. In this technological age people tend not to read as much as they used too. Designers have to make reading a much more pleasurable experience by providing as many visuals as possible. I would take that a step further by replacing textual context with visuals as long as it doesn't compromise the clarity of the information.

433 CONTRAST AND RHYTHM CREATE INTEREST. Contrast dark with bright, loud with quiet, fast with slow, complex with simple, etc. The rhythm of the contrast is very important. It constitutes the order in which the design elements create visual play without creating anxiety for the viewer.

434 LET THE RESEARCH LEAD YOUR CREATIVITY, AND DON'T LET YOUR CREATIVITY LEAD YOUR RESEARCH. The worst mistake designers make is to formulate preconceived ideas as soon as they read the brief. These limit design to the predictable. Inspiration comes from everywhere, and that's why it's highly recommendable to research first and to make this research as broad as possible. Idea making starts after having researched everything about the subject, product, and campaign.

435 READ, READ, READ. And by reading I don't mean just design books, I mean any kind of reading. What comes out of our heads is nothing but a result of what we put in it. Reading enriches our imagination and makes our ideation process far more sophisticated.

436 LISTEN TO MUSIC WHILE WORKING. Music is one of the greatest inspirations that designers use. Besides getting inspired, music reduces the sense of design's heavy, slow pace. Consequently it allows us to stay for a longer time working on a project. I prefer a slow beat when I'm working. It's important to still be able to think as you work, loud music can get distracting.

437 EXHAUST YOUR OPTIONS. We always tend to fall back on what we know, repeating ourselves over and over. The best work comes usually after throwing out the first ten attempts. Usually those are the ten solutions that you have experimented with in the past and they are safe. Reach beyond your comfort zone.

438 DESIGNER'S BLOCK HAPPENS VERY OFTEN AND YOU SHOULDN'T LET IT STOP YOU. The best work comes after major blocks. The best way to deal with designer's block is to step away from the computer and do something else. I personally think that reading helps a lot, I completely stop thinking about my project when I read. On the other hand every time I step away from my block and read, I find something in my reading that inspires me and solves my problem.

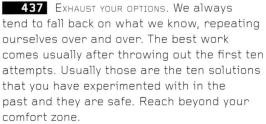

439 "DON'T TRY TO BE ORIGINAL, JUST TRY TO BE GOOD" (PAUL RAND). As depressing as it sounds, everything has been done, so don't try to make it original, just try to make it good. If you happen to come up with something original as you're going through your process, it will all be added value.

440
God is in the details. Details are what set the good designer apart from the incredible designer. Well-composed artwork will make a strong impression. The subtle details draw the viewer closer, maintaining viewer curiosity Details are very much like spices: you can't really taste them on their own when used in food, but once they're missing, the recipe loses its flavor.

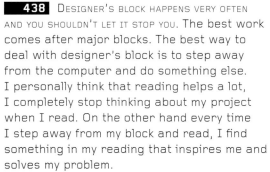

441 BALANCE. Keeping centered is everything. At every stage of the design process ask yourself if the choices you made and make are in balance with the rest. A strong and winning design is the result of perfectly balanced ingredients, just like cooking.

442 STORYTELLING. Start with a story. What story do you want to tell, to what audience? The design is a logical consequence of this story, not the other way around.

443 INSPIRATION. Seek it everywhere and always. One source is copying, a thousand sources is inspiration. Your search for inspiration needs to have insane proportions.

444 IDEA. Share them—they are not yours anyway. An idea is a sum of parts, you're only the collector, the composer of these parts.

445 COLLABORATE. One plus one is three, the outcome is bigger than the sum of the parts. By collaborating you will see new shades, new ways of thinking, new directions and together you will create new destinations.

446 VISIBILITY. The web has endless possibilities to promote your work, share your thoughts and create a world you want to work and live in.

447 RELEVANT. Make it relevant. To make a bottle black to give it a premium feel is easy, but it will not work when the story behind it is missing. Always ask yourself and your client: "Why?"

448 LOVE. Do the things you love or create love for the things you do. Don't accept jobs where you will not learn something you can use to reach your goals. It's better to do the worst job in the best place, than the best job in the worst place.

449 CELEBRATE. Celebrate the things you do, see it as a gift and be curious with all your senses to what may come. And be thankful to your network, they have brought you there. The future is yours!

450
Write down your goals—what do you want to achieve in one year, in five and in ten years. You can't reach your destination without a proper direction plan.

Joachim Baan

www.anothercompany.org

Joachim Baan is a graphic designer and photographer working under the name Anothercompany operating in art, fashion, and communication. In his own words: "For me, positivity and a never ending hunger for the aesthetic are the main ingredients of my work and life; get inspired and inspire people to stay hungry, to take that extra step forward and explore new realms." His expertise spans many fields, as shown in his projects: an identity for Paris-based fashion photographer Tom Watson; the interior photography of the card-box office of the Amsterdam-based advertising company Nothing; the identity, branding, and interior concept for Tenue de Nîmes, a denim-inspired boutique and label at the Elandsgracht, Amsterdam; and project photography for Nike.

K.J. Kim

www.kjkimdesign.com

A Chicago-based graphic designer, K.J. Kim studied Visual Design in Seoul as an undergraduate and later focused on information graphics and environment-communication design for her master's at SAIC. Her thesis investigated graphical representation of the translation of languages, both verbal and non-verbal. Also interested in the more conceptual side of graphic design, she has been featured in several exhibitions and has worked on various visual commutation areas. Under her belt is experience in the print department at VSA Partners, at The Chicago History Museum in the exhibition design department, and at Perkins and Will in the Branded Environment. Her latest projects include brochure design for the SAIC and the Day/Night typeface design.

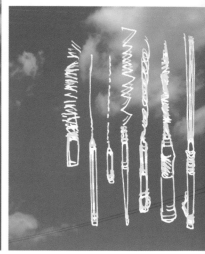

451 Colors are always great whatever they are. Only combination matters.

452 I love clips! They organize my work really well.

453 Use all different kinds of pens. Using a different pen is like wearing different clothes everyday.

454 Visit art supplies stores once a while; they have all the colors/ideas/textures of the world.

455
GROW A PLANT!

456 Collect ideas in a secret red envelope: they usually come out when you don't need them. So write them down and save them for later.

457 Try to talk to someone who isn't a graphic designer.

458 Always sketch: my right hand knows my ideas the best.

459 Try to do something totally different; sports, writing stories, etc.

460 Open the window. Inhale. Exhale.

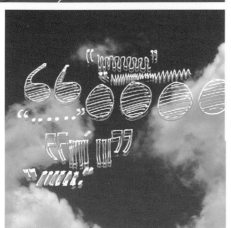

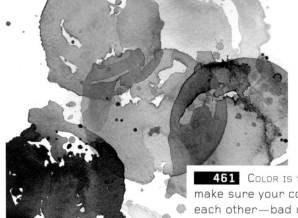

HEY LADIES

SOCIAL MIX

461 COLOR IS YOUR FRIEND! But make sure your colors complement each other—bad use of color can ruin your design or illustration.

462 DON'T LET YOUR CLIENTS SUCK THE LIFE OUT OF YOU AND YOUR PROJECTS. Always listen to your instincts—if you have a bad feeling about a client, you may need to walk away.

463 BE SOCIAL. Attending social events and networking can help you meet new people and bring in new clients.

464 NEVER STOP LEARNING. If you think you already know everything, you're wrong.

465 HOP ON THE SOUL TRAIN. Listening to music while you work can help get you in the creative zone.

sucker.

Learn

all heart, **ALL** passion.

USE BIG TYPE

466 BE PASSIONATE ABOUT YOUR CAREER AND STRIVE TO GET BETTER. If you don't have passion for design, you're probably in the wrong profession.

467 WHEN ALL ELSE FAILS, use BIG type.

468 DON'T WASTE THE DAY AWAY. Be efficient with your time and schedule small goals you want to accomplish throughout the day.

469 SHOW YOUR FUNNY SIDE THROUGH YOUR WORK. People react to humor!

WAKE UP

470
BE INSPIRED BY THINGS FROM YOUR PAST. Anything that reminds me of my childhood is a huge source of inspiration to me.

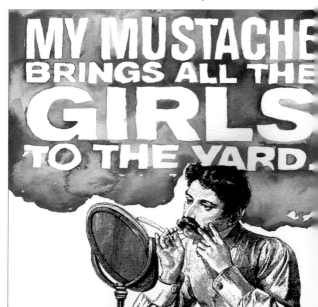

MY MUSTACHE BRINGS ALL THE GIRLS TO THE YARD.

Karen Kurycki

www.cmykaren.com

Based in Jacksonville, Florida, Karen Kurycki is an art director/ illustrator. Design is her passion and she loves to combine illustration with design in her commercial work. She has been experimenting with watercolor since her days at Kent State University, embracing its unpredictability and the surprises that can come out of using it. She admits that in her view of the world she usually sees the humorous, the quirky, the slightly off "normal." Karen is an active member of AIGA, the professional association for design, and in her spare time enjoys collecting random 80s paraphernalia and singing karaoke. Her latest projects include the AIGA Design Connection poster, N.S. Print campaign posters, and posters for the band The Helio Sequence.

Kind Company

www.kindcompany.com

A two person, independent web and print design office in Brooklyn, New York. Since 2004, partners Patricia Belen and Greg D'Onofrio have been using design as a tool to help small to medium sized businesses communicate their ideas, products, and services. From art galleries to non-profit associations, restaurants to retailers or entrepreneurs to online companies; good design is simple, smart, and usable—a balance of function and aesthetics. Through design, they establish the client's communication of their messages in an honest and meaningful way. Some of their latest projects are: Glenn Horowitz bookseller and art gallery (a website to communicate a growing number of contemporary exhibits), and Sauce restaurant (a visual identity to communicate a contemporary twist on the classic Italian restaurant).

Neue Grafik
New Graphic Design
Graphisme actuel

471 Discover graphic design pioneers and the context of their contributions.

472 Keep things orderly and sensible—design with a grid.

473 Become intimate with a typeface.

474 Organize, clarify, and make information accessible.

475 Function first.

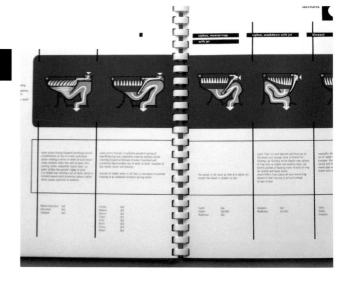

476 Design with objectivity, purpose, and relevance.

477 Use graphic design as a communication tool to solve problems, deliver solutions.

478 Maintain clarity and precision while being playful and stylistic.

479 Live to work. Believe in good graphic design.

A sign systems manual

Crosby/Fletcher/Forbes

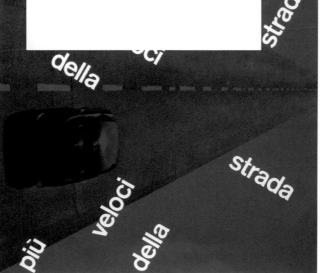

480
SIMPLE IS DIFFICULT.

481	Less Answers	More Questions
482	Less E-mail	More Dialogue
483	Less Ego	More Team
484	Less Wrapping	More Content
485	Less Medium	More Message

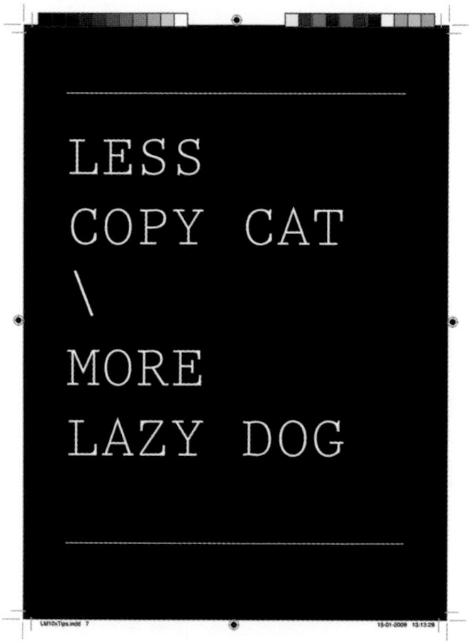

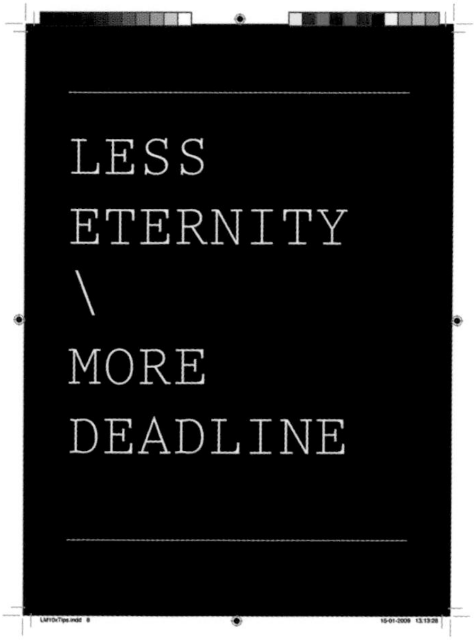

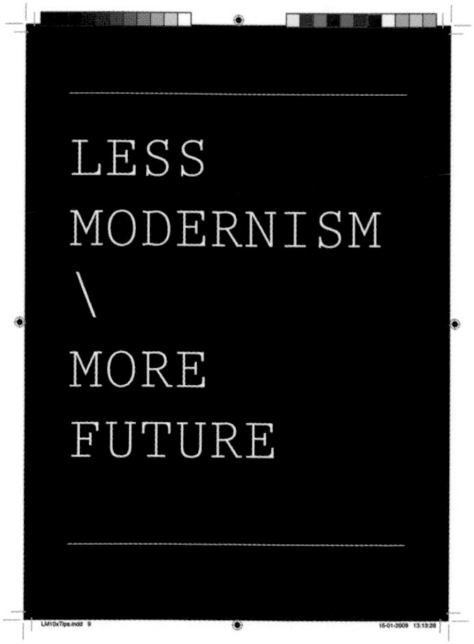

LESS
READYMADE
\
MORE
HANDMADE

LESS
COPY CAT
\
MORE
LAZY DOG

LESS
ETERNITY
\
MORE
DEADLINE

LESS
MODERNISM
\
MORE
FUTURE

LESS
HEAVEN
\
MORE
VOID

486	Less Readymade	More Handmade
487	Less Copy cat	More Lazy dog
488	Less Eternity	More Deadline
489	Less Modernism	More Future
490	Less Heaven	More Void

Lesley Moore

www.lesley-moore.nl

Lesley Moore is an Amsterdam-based graphic design agency, founded in May 2004 by Karin van den Brandt (Blerick, the Netherlands) and Alex Clay (Lørenskog, Norway). Both studied at the Arnhem Academy of the Arts (the Netherlands). Current clients include: BIS publishers, Centraal Museum Utrecht, Wilfried Lentz, *Mark Magazine*, MTV, *De Volkskrant* (Gorilla, in collaboration with Herman van Bostelen and De Designpolitie) and Warmoesmarkt. Lesley Moore have a curious way of defining their identity: the LM Logo Machine project.

The future Lesley Moore identity is created by... anyone. Friends, family, colleagues, clients or strangers are asked to create a logo and thus make a contribution to Lesley Moore's ever changing corporate identity. The logos are stored in an apposite logo bank and used for each new project.

Librito

www.librito.de

Florian Zietz is the mind behind Librito, a small design company with multiple years of experience located in Hamburg. The company specializes in logos, corporate identity, packaging, brochures, books, calligraphy, typography, and (lately) type design. Librito combines strategy and creativity to develop successful and effective solutions for their clients. The illustrative multilayer font FF Headz, published by FontFont.com received a Certificate of Excellence in Type Design from the Type Directors Club in New York in 2006.

Some of their projects include: e-books for iPod Touch and iPhone, a final year balance for Energiekontor AG, identity design for Kinderhaus Stenvort, and Naturheil-praxis, Zansibar and Segmenta font design.

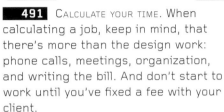

491 CALCULATE YOUR TIME. When calculating a job, keep in mind, that there's more than the design work: phone calls, meetings, organization, and writing the bill. And don't start to work until you've fixed a fee with your client.

492 WORK PROPERLY RIGHT FROM THE BEGINNING. You will save a lot of time on the final artwork—and it's easier for anyone else you're collaborating with.

493 ASK QUESTIONS. If you have questions about the job, don't hesitate to discuss the matter with your client. Your client will appreciate that you're interested and trying to work efficiently.

494 LEARN TO THINK IN ALTERNATIVES. There's always more than one way to solve a problem. Instead of sticking to the very first idea and refining that approach, come up with two or three alternative solutions.

495 COMMON DAY INSPIRATION. Make notes of interesting visual structures or ideas—e.g. with pen and sketchbook, your mobile phone camera, or something else. It's a great source of inspiration.

496 COLLECT THINGS. I have a box with things I found at the beach, at the flea market, and anywhere else. This box is like a playground and helps me to come up with ideas. It's also great to make nice collages.

497 Get inspirations from other areas of daily life, like children's games, music, literature, street art. For example, use the structure of a children's pop-up or a surrealist game to develop a typeface.

498 IF NOTHING WORKS OUT, PLAY SPORTS. It's good for your health and helps to relax. Some of my best ideas came while I was jogging.

499 Always back up your files.

500

RANDOM PAGE INSPIRATION. If you're stuck with a design, open a magazine at random and start working with an element you find there: a font, a color, a structure, a grid, etc.

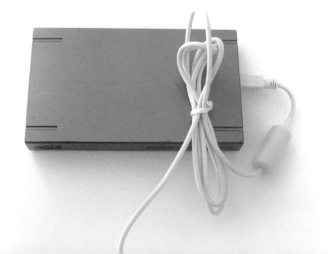

501 Invest time in ideas. They keep graphic design alive and dancing on its toes.

502 If an idea or direction isn't at once evident, recognize when to stop forcing it. Ideas can't be pushed. Trust the process. You'll very rarely fail to come up with the goods.

503 At the beginning surround yourself with visual inspiration and lovely new pencils.

504 Learn how to edit where necessary. But don't tear out pages and try not to rub out.

505 Gather. Believe in collecting things, even if the reason for keeping something isn't immediately clear.

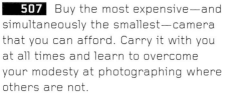

506 Create a system in your collection. Find the way that works for you.

507 Buy the most expensive—and simultaneously the smallest—camera that you can afford. Carry it with you at all times and learn to overcome your modesty at photographing where others are not.

508 Don't ever stop looking. If you can't see anymore, change the scene.

509 Go places and talk to people.

510 When regarding your work, always ask yourself: "What am I trying to say?"

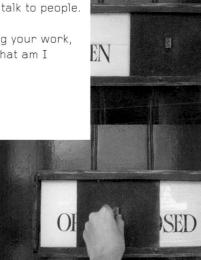

Lizzie Ridout

www.lizzieridout.com, www.artsparklets.co.uk

UK-based designer Lizzie Ridout tends to avoid working in one particular discipline, believing instead that the form of any one outcome should be suggested by the theme or idea at its heart. The majority of her work stems from a desire to discover: a fact, a story, an object, an image, a ritual, a process, a history. These discoveries then inspire projects that borrow working methods from graphic design, fine art, and illustration. She graduated from the Royal College of Art in 2002 and has since been involved in various commissioned and self-initiated projects. Lizzie has exhibited nationally and internationally and is currently working on new folios for her publication *Homeward Bound*, whilst also lecturing at University College Falmouth and the University of Plymouth.

Lowres

www.lowres.nl

Amsterdam-based Jop Quirindongo is the man behind Lowres, his trademark and digital alter ego. Originally educated in interactive media conceptualizing at the Hogeschool voor de Kunsten Utrecht and Portsmouth University, Jop developed himself as an all-around creative with a broad experience ranging from advertising art-direction, photography, inter-active graphic design, and music. His latest projects include: Blidfrukt Vit—concept and visualization for a Swedish wine brand, digital illustrations for Freemagenta.nl and *De Volkskrant*, identity and packaging design for Tremolo Recordings, a minisite for the introduction of the Nissan 350Z, identity and packaging design for Carnal Records, Polar State Records, and Phenom Records, and an honorary mention for a book cover design contest.

THINK BEFORE YOU START.
A BUNCH OF TYPE FACES, COLOR
ARE NOTHING WITHOUT AN IDEA

01

DON'T ALWAYS
FOLLOW
THE
RULES.

(and this is not a rule!)

GO

Breathe!

START ALL OVER AGAIN

WHE

IDEA

05

511   Be nice to people.

512   Breathe. Don't overestimate
the power of design. Oxygen is much
more important.

513   Don't show your clients the
proposals you're not fully happy with.
They will like them.

514   Do a lot of other
creative stuff like making music or
photography. Sooner or later it will
all come together.

515   Look around you. Design is
in everything.

03

04

DO A LOT OF OTHER CREATIVE
STUFF LIKE MAKING MUSIC OR
PHOTOGRAPHY. SOONER OR
LATER IT WILL ALL COME
TOGETHER

And it's
FUN

D SHAPES

PUT SO

LOOK AROUND YOU DESIGN IS IN EVERYTHIN

LOOK AROUND YOU

07

↑ UP

THERE

look!

NEXT PAGE

A LOT OF TIME IN YOUR WORK AND ALSO IN THE WAY YOU'RE PRESENTING YOUR WORK

06

516 Do stuff your own way. It will always give you the best result.

517 Don't always follow the rules.

518 When you're stuck on an idea start all over again.

519 Go. Think before you start. A bunch of typefaces, colors, and shapes are nothing without an idea.

520 Put a lot of time in your work and also in the way you're presenting your work.

NICE TO PEOPLE

100 FREE

08

09

Don't show your client the proposals you're not fully happy with.

They wi like thei

ONE WAY

10

DO STUFF YOUR OWN WAY.

FOR EXAMPLE: THIS SMALL

521 ENTERTAIN THEM. Beauty is a concept that depends on current trends, while irony isn't. Graphic designers have the possibility to play with concepts through images and forms, even when they do it in a subtle way. It's that understated ludic element that sparks awe and interest in the viewer's eye. Most people are bored and look for emotions.

522 LOOK ELSEWHERE. Being up-to-date with the state of the art of graphic design is important, but there is also a danger of homologation. Today's designers should be active in society as content creators. If the content you propose in your work is self-referential it will turn out to be redundant and sterile. Search for ideas in books, exhibits, in travels, folklore, under the ground and in the toolbox. While you're at it turn off your computer, your head will work better.

523 LOOK FOR A RATIONALE. Every communication project starts with a problem and ends with a valid solution. This is why we need a rationale for every decision, it will not only help you motivate your line of reasoning but it will also help you to focus on the objectives. Back in university I once found myself completely unprepared for a scenography project. I improvised a terrible scenery with my shirt and other found objects. The professor's only comment was: "If you are able to justify your choices in a serious, satisfying and coherent way, then it's good." A lesson to remember.

524 TAKE HEED OF WHAT HAPPENS AROUND YOU. Reality that surrounds you is often more incredible than fantasy. Me and my business partner were trying to find a name for our newborn magazine. Lars, our German roommate at the time, had a poor grasp of Italian, but a capacity of inter-synthesis between the languages he spoke that made him the perfect candidate to study to come up with something original. And in fact, he gave us a great idea. Why not combine the English word "cool" with the Italian adjective suffix "-issimo?" The name was perfect; it was exotic enough, and balanced between the phonetic resemblances with the Italian slang word for "luck."

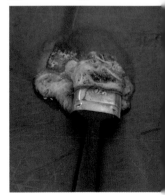

525 PERFECTION DOESN'T EXIST. Vincent de Rijk's studio (www.vincentderijk.nl) makes beautifully detailed mock-ups for the biggest names of worldwide architecture. He's an advocate of aiming for perfection in design, but at the same time, he believes that imperfection breeds the most interesting particulars.

526 NETWORKING IS IMPORTANT, AND SO IS RECOGNIZING ONE'S LIMITS. Surround yourself with people you like and of whom you respect the work and ideas. Your work environment is vital to your quality of life and consequently to the outcome and quality of your projects. Often an assignment will require the work of more than one professional figure. Don't be seduced by the malicious idea of "do-it-all-yourself;" it's always better to divide more work between talented individuals.

527 CREATE A REAL-LIFE WORKING MODEL AS A BENCHMARK. This will help you to avoid wasting time on fallacious solutions and to better the overall outcome of the project.

528 DON'T DESIGN ANOTHER MONSTER. Your predecessors have already generated enough even for your descendants.

529 WHEN IT'S NOT NECESSARY, turn off your computer and have fun.

530
LEARN TO PLAY CHESS. STRATEGY IS IMPORTANT. As a contract worker or a freelancer you'll have to deal with other people's ideas. All of them will try to steer the project towards their own visualization, and frankly, some people's visual taste is terrible. Diplomacy is key; sometimes it's useful to dribble the question, because stubbornness doesn't help. Try to get to know the person or people you have to work with, learn to negotiate, and earn their trust. While proposing a visual identity for the township of Ravenna, we encountered resistance from our client, suggesting that our proposal—two boxers facing each other—was too chauvinistic. We resolved the question noting that the township coat of arms was also a perfect graphical solution for the problem. In fact it represented two lions in the exact same posture as our boxers—with the exception that it was impossible for the client to reject!

Luca Bendandi
www.brembo.tumblr.com

Luca Bendandi was born in Romagna, land of freaks, geniuses, and crazy folk. He kept a healthy balance up until university, when he abandoned water polo and started dedicating himself to all of social life's derivations. He loves art, beauty (especially if feminine), and rock and roll. A strong opposer of nuclear energy, he adores tomatoes and cooking. When he realized that designers weren't prized (or paid) in his native provincial town he decided to discover the world, working with Estudi Mariscal in Barcelona, Vincent de Rijk in Rotterdam, and Mario Piazza in Milan. In between his European roaming he found the time to found two magazines alongside fellow designer Gianluca Achilli: *Coolissimo* and *quiNDI*. He is now art director for *Rutas del Mundo* and *Penthouse Spain*; the latter assignment makes all his friends happy.

MacGregor Harp

www.pnmnl.com

A designer living and working in Brooklyn, New York. He primarily works in motion graphics, broadcast graphics, print design, and interactive/experience design. Some of his projects are: W/ (opening show for a new gallery in New York), SuperVision (a silkscreened poster for The Builders Associations production of SuperVision at the REDCAT theater in Los Angeles), Earthquakes and Aftershocks (a collection of Calarts posters from 1986 to 2004). His work is often spontaneous and makes use of simple, inexpensive elements. The De Koonig exchange—a poster, printed in an edition of twenty-four in black and white, was enriched with added color with simple stencils and spray paint. Celebrating the extemporaneousness of design, this project, designed during a trip to the Netherlands, was designed on a laptop in several bars over Easter weekend.

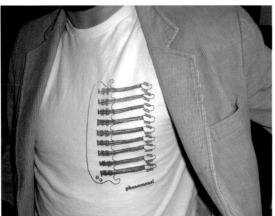

531 I've noticed graphic design is a LOT different when you're in school. Especially art school.

532 It can be egotistical, but it really shouldn't be.

533 It can be social...and seems like it used to be.

534 I got snippy with an art director one time because I didn't like the colors she was using. I felt really silly later.

535 Clients rarely seem to want to hear about typography.

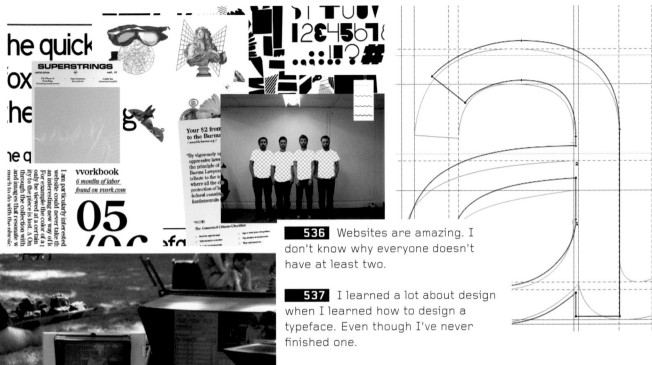

536 Websites are amazing. I don't know why everyone doesn't have at least two.

537 I learned a lot about design when I learned how to design a typeface. Even though I've never finished one.

538 I have gotten some of my best gigs over instant messenger.

539 Everyone loves a laugh.

540 I've never gotten anything from asking for it through voicemail.

541 USUALLY, RESEARCH. I start by doing research. Subsequently, I brainstorm and write down key words. In the beginning of a project I like to sit down by my desk and just think of various concepts and opportunities. At this stage, I generally think of the project 24/7, everywhere I go. It is surprising how much inspiration you can get by just walking around in a city and observing your surroundings. Vibrant cities are a great source of inspiration. Additionally, I get a lot of inspiration by socializing and doing things I enjoy, such as dancing. It makes me unwind.

542 TIMELINES. In the first part of the brief (including research and initial sketches), I find it a bit difficult to adhere to a strict timeline, as I believe that this is one of the most vital parts in the process, and its duration often varies. But if I were to divide the whole project into two parts, research/concept and execution, I would say that in average, I would spend about 80% on the research and creating a strong concept, and 20% on the design. For me, the design comes almost naturally when I have a strong concept in place. I also keep a diary of my work and of how many hours I put into a project, in order to be able to effectively plan the next one.

543 UNDERSTANDING. For me, it is important to get a clear understanding of what the client wants. Initially, I start conducting research through using books, the Internet, browsing stores, etc. Walking into the store where, for instance, the product is sold really helps create a better picture of how it looks in the actual environment. I like having substantial facts and background information about the client and the brief before starting the design execution.

544 KEYWORDS. I usually draft the first ideas by writing down keywords in a mixture of English and Swedish, similarly to a mind map. I find it useful, as it gives a clear picture of the various parts of the project and the different paths you can take. It's then easy to decide what routes appear to be the strongest ones to present to the client.

545 TOOLS. The most common tools I use are: pen/pencil, paper, rubber, knife, ruler, double sided tape, and my computer (Photoshop, Illustrator, and InDesign).

MONDAY _ Research/S
TUESDAY _ Research + iv
              /2h
WEDNESDAY_
THURSDAY_
FRIDAY _
SATURDAY_
SUNDAY_

546 NOT NECESSARILY A MESS. I prefer order within a mess. I am not a big fan of having lots of things on my desk, but I like having things around me to draw inspiration from, such as posters and cut out papers on my walls. I like working in a light room with lots of space around me.

547 FOLLOW A STRICT GRID SYSTEM. But I find it more exciting to break it (if I've got a good reason to do so). When designing I like to use a modular grid. It gives me better control over the layout.

548 I WOULD LIKE TO RECOMMEND *SustainAble*, by Aaris Sherin. It is a handbook about environmentally conscious graphic design. The book features information about the latest materials and techniques needed to reach sustainable design solutions. *SustainAble* has been a great inspiration source for me, as I aim to work in the most environmentally friendly way possible.

549 CARE ABOUT YOUR PORTFOLIO. I care a lot about the way my work is presented, as this in turn represents me as a designer. Essentially, it is about communicating who you are as a designer to people who aren't familiar with you or your work. For me, a poorly presented portfolio denotes a designer that does not value his/her own work. I like presenting my work in a simplistic manner, as I believe that the work should be in focus. The three keywords would be "less is more."

550 DANCE. I HAVE BEEN DOING GYMNASTICS and dancing my whole life. It really helps me calm down mentally, which improves my creativity as I'm doing something I love. Additionally, it gives me time to think of something other than design and completely forget about work.

Malin Holmström
www.malinholmstrom.com

A graphic designer who has mostly been working on identity, packaging, and print. Malin was born in a small town in Sweden, and later moved to Australia to study design. She received her Bachelor degree in Communication Design in December 2008. One could say that her style reflects her radical latitude shift—a traceable nordic sobriety afloats in a more playful use of color and concept, reflecting the warm lifestyle of the New South Wales coast. One of Malin's latest projects is Survey catalog, a booklet designed to enlighten people about household sustainable living. It also raises awareness of the need to minimize natural resource consumption. The catalog is bound with a rubber band, 100 percent recyclable when removed, and it comes in a compostable bubble plastic wrap especially researched for the project.

Margus Tamm
www.tammtamm.net

After studying Printmaking Arts and obtaining a MA in Interdisciplinary Arts, Margus is now a PhD fellow at the Eesti Kunstiakadeemia Tartu (Estonian Academy of Arts). His research topic is Interventionism (known also as tactical media or culture jamming or neo-situationism or artivism or post-activism). Along with graphic design he is also a performance/installation artist and a university lecturer. His work experience encompasses 12 years as an art director in different advertising agencies Publicis, Young and Rubicam, DDB. Moreover, thanks to his doctoral project he has become increasingly interested in critical writing and curatorial practices—recently curating Artishok Annual Exhibition, presenting an overview of emerging younger generation Estonian art, arranged under the aegis of the art and criticism blog Artishok.

551 BE THE CLIENT; MAKE THE PROJECT. I make designs for my own exhibitions, for events organized by my friends, for the parties I'm planning to visit. Most of the projects viewed on my homepage, are self-initiated projects.

552 BE INVOLVED. If you are involved in arranging the event and the design for it, those two can evolve as parallels, supporting and supplementing each other. If graphic design bounds with just illustrative functions, this can be considered as under-usage of design potential.

553 BE TRUE TO GRAPHIC DESIGN. I don't see anything controversial in self-initiated projects. As I see it, graphic design is an independent semantic discipline with its own inner logic. And that means that there are also problems raised only by the discipline itself and questions to be answered only inside this discipline. Graphic design does not always have to present something else to be itself.

554 TRY TO DESIGN FOR DIFFERENT SETTINGS. After all, all is one. For example, when working intensely with some art project, it is usual that during this process I get also some design ideas as side effects. And vice versa, some ideas that were counted out during the design process may become useful in another art project. And it's equally as rewarding. But that doesn't mean that design is art. Design is design. There may not be a difference for myself but the end results go to different boxes.

555 EXPAND YOUR BORDERS. I find multidisciplinarity quite interesting and inspiring and I'll never erase borders between different roles or different disciplines, because these can serve as very effective tools.

556 DESIGN WITH LESS. Because most of my projects are non-budgetary, the less expensive media is also the favorite one. Sometimes we're talking about the possibilities offered by copy-machine. On one hand it is a practical necessity, on the other creating from limited possibilities is also a conceptual choice: the playground is smaller, more basic and more complicated, but the end result will also be stronger, because it carries both aesthetical and practical arguments. That makes design look somehow inevitable.

557 COMMUNICATE. Use Skype!

558 GET STARTED EASILY. With doodling and googling.

559 KEEP WORKING. It may take many miles of walking in your room before you get somewhere. Then you stop and start digging, until you finally find something. If it makes you feel happy then it is the right thing. Then you show it to your significant others. Then it's ready.

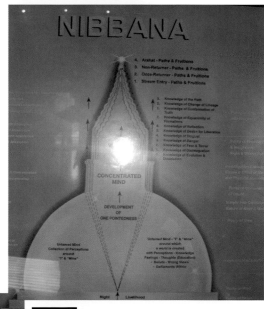

560 NEVER LOOK BACK. One day before the deadline, when everything is finished and just waiting to be published you reach the point where everything you've made seems weak and pointless and you feel great tension to remake everything. Don't.

561 MUSIC/ART/LITERATURE/CINEMA. Respectively: Radiohead/Francis Bacon/ José Saramago/David Lynch.

562 AS A DESIGNER YOU SHOULD READ. And not only design books: try *White Noise* by Don DeLillo. It's a funny and interesting commentary on consumerism.

563 IGNORE YOUR SURROUNDINGS WHILE WORKING. My workspace changes drastically from the beginning to the end of a project. I start with a clean, super-organized desk, but by the end it's always littered with piles of printouts and used coffee cups.

564 SMART, BUT SNEAKER-Y. I dress relatively casual for interviews and client meetings. I usually wear jeans and a button-up shirt. For more formal meetings, I'll wear dress shoes, but usually I wear sneakers.

INT ROD UCT ION

Latin America is a place of great economic disparity. Its rich are amongst the world's wealthiest, while its poor lead some of the most miserable lives on the planet. Gated communities full of BMWs and private yachts overlook shanty towns constructed out of garbage. The small group of economic elite enjoy comfortable lives where they must struggle with decisions like whether to fly to Miami or New York for their next shopping trip. They are the families who for generations have controlled the governments of South America. They are the descendents of the conquerors who raped and pillaged the continent and just like their ancestors, these privileged few have very little interest in the lives of those who reside in its slums. It is of no concern to them if people are hungry, illiterate, or if they make a fair wage. What matters is maintaining the status quo. They do this by instituting policies that only benefit the rich, by laundering money from the government, and catering to foreign investors at the expense of its own people.

In the decades following World War 2, socialist, nationalist, and populist movements began to spread throughout the continent; groups of people who said, "No more," to the disparities, and the corruption. The people began to assemble, and demanded their struggles be heard. These movements grew and grew, and in Chile they even elected a socialist president. Salvador Allende became president in 1970. He won on a platform that promised agrarian reform, public work projects, and free milk for all Chilean children. The success of these movements terrified both the Latin American oligarchy and the United States, who felt that their economic interests in the regions were threatened. The United States' relationship with Latin America is a very lucrative one. For centuries, in exchange for a small percentage of profits, Latin American countries have allowed U.S. corporations to install facilities on the continent and take advantage of low costs and next to non existent labor laws. These new social movements were threatening to not only change South America's power structure, but to reform the laws that were advantageous to American business. The two groups decided to take action to stop the potential changes.

On September 11th, 1973, Salvador Allende's democratically elected government was overthrown. Led by General Agusto Pinochet, and funded by the U.S., the military stormed the presidential palace, killing Allende, and claimed control of the country. The new government immediately began a campaign to rid Chile of subversives. This not only included armed rebel groups, b

565 GRIDS ARE NECESSARY. Absolutely. 100% of the time.

566 FONTS. I despise Copperplate. It's so ugly and clunky, yet it's impossible to go a day without seeing it on a restaurant menu or a storefront window.

567 MORE THAN CMYK. I used nothing but CMYK, but lately I've been playing around with earth tones. Right now I'm working on a poster where I only use different shades of brown.

568 AUTO-ADVERTISE. I've received a lot of publicity by submitting my portfolio to design blogs. It's an easy (and free) way of getting your name out there.

569 LESS IS MORE. I think design has the biggest impact when it can communicate its message without superfluous elements.

570 Love letterpress. The tactile quality of pressed type.

UGLY

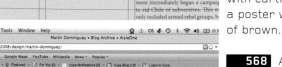

File Edit View History Bookmarks Tools Window Help

http://www.aisleone.net/2008/design/martin-dominguez/

Apple Yahoo Google Maps YouTube Wikipedia News▾ Popular▾

AisleOne

An inspirational resource focused on graphic design, typography, grid systems, minimalism and modernism.

Shop Wallpapers About Contact

is entry

currently reading "Martin Dominguez", an AisleOne

09.25.08 / 11am

Design, International Typographic Style

ck & white, graphic design, International ahic Style, minimalism, modernism, Music

igation

owing/Barcelona

itories »

Martin Dominguez

Joy Division. Love Will
Tear Us Apart. 1979

00:00

00:30
Love, Love Will Tear Us Apart, Again.

01:00
Love, Love Will

01:30
Tear Us Apart, Again.

02:00
Love, Love Will

02:30
Tear Us Apart. Love, Love Will Tear Us Apart, Again.

Here's a sweet poster by Martin Dominguez that charts each instrument in the song Love Will Tear Us Apart by Joy Division.

Man, this song is definitely popular with graphic designers.

ments

ment form | comments rss [1] | trackback url [1]

Martin Dominguez

www.dominguezdesign.net

American designer Martin Dominguez is first and foremost a print designer, with a particular interest in editorial design. He received a degree in graphic design from the University of Delaware. His work is heavily influenced by mid-twentieth-century Swiss design. From his work it's evident how there are few things he likes better than how big and bold sans serifs look on a page. His love expands to grids, white space, and Helvetica Neue 85 Heavy. Latest projects include: *The Original War on Terror*—a book detailing the horrors of the dictatorships that ruled the cone of South America during the 70s and 80s and the acclaimed *Love Will Tear Us Apart*—a poster charting each instrument on a second by second basis in the song by the seminal band Joy Division.

Matteo Astolfi

www.teoasto.it

Born in the fabulous 70s, after a happy childhood in Santarcangelo di Romagna, he moved to the grey and ugly Milan to study Industrial Design at the Politecnico, giving up a probable career in professional baseball. After some funny-hard-crazy years full of *negroni* in the city of design, he received his degree and started working as a visual designer for Domus Academy, then for Leftloft and as teaching assistant. Meanwhile, Matteo kept interest alive with freelance and self-initiated projects. During these years he discovered the world of infographics for newspapers and magazines developing a healthy interest in this field. Nevertheless, during all this time photography grew preponderant in his interests and made him relocate to Barcelona to move his first steps as a professional.

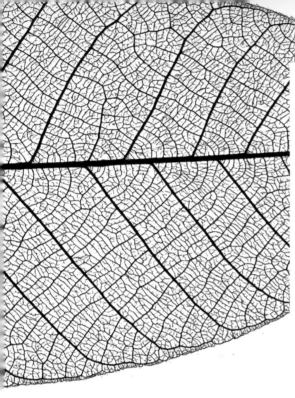

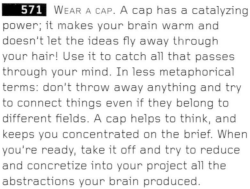

571 WEAR A CAP. A cap has a catalyzing power; it makes your brain warm and doesn't let the ideas fly away through your hair! Use it to catch all that passes through your mind. In less metaphorical terms: don't throw away anything and try to connect things even if they belong to different fields. A cap helps to think, and keeps you concentrated on the brief. When you're ready, take it off and try to reduce and concretize into your project all the abstractions your brain produced.

572 TAKE A REST. Sometimes we need to rest to let our brain reorganize all the material we put in the cap (see previous tip!). So, take a siesta, sleep half an hour, or if you can't do it take a walk on the beach or in an open space where your eyes can follow the line of horizon. You'll see how it's healthy and productive in the long run.

573 TURN IT OFF! Never start a project in front of a computer screen! No way. Turn it off and just start "analogically" thinking.

574 DON'T GO FOR ORIGINALITY AT ALL COSTS. As Jim Jarmush says: "Nothing is original." Steal from anywhere that resonates with inspiration or fuels your imagination. Devour old films, new films, music, books, paintings, photographs, poems, dreams, random conversations, architecture, bridges, street signs, trees, clouds, bodies of water, light, and shadows. Select only things to steal from that speak directly to your soul. If you do this, your work (and theft) will be authentic. Authenticity is invaluable; originality is non-existent. And don't bother concealing your thievery—celebrate it if you feel like it. In any case, always remember what Jean-Luc Godard said: "It's not where you take things from—it's where you take them to."

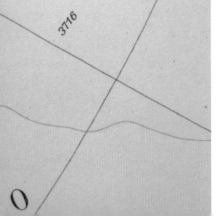

Fuori
Santarcangelo
dei Teatri

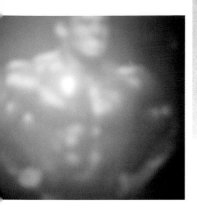

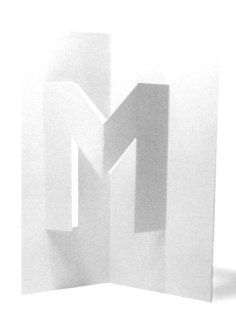

575 BE BRAVE. Listening to advice or other's opinions is always a good habit, but remember that you are the only master of your work and if you want it to be authentic and coherent you have to make your own decisions. Otherwise you will feel like it doesn't belong to your sensibility and style.

576 EVERYBODY IS A VISUAL DESIGNER. Compromises with clients are the daily grind; everybody feels that they can do our job and tell us which color or font to use. So, defend your professionalism! If you're weak on these aspects, go take a course in dialectics in Athens or get a Doberman!

577 COHERENCE/INCOHERENCE. Being coherent is important.. but incoherence also plays a role. Disaccording elements can at times give life to a project.

578 LESS AESTHETICS, MORE ETHICS*. Don't be boring and self-indulgent. Graphic design is important, it's everywhere. So use it well, do it well.
*This was the claim of the 2000 Venice Architecture Biennale.

579 TABULA RASA. If you take a way and then notice, after some work, it isn't the right one, don't keep going on with it. Don't be stubborn. Throw your sketch into the trash and start with a new blank one ready to be filled with good ideas.

580
THINK IN SUBTRACTION. Most of the time designers add things on things, visually and conceptually—even when they have concepts. My opinion is that we should proceed in a different (opposite) way: subtracting. Simplify and try to focus on the message, but that doesn't mean being explicit—try to communicate directly in a symbolic way.

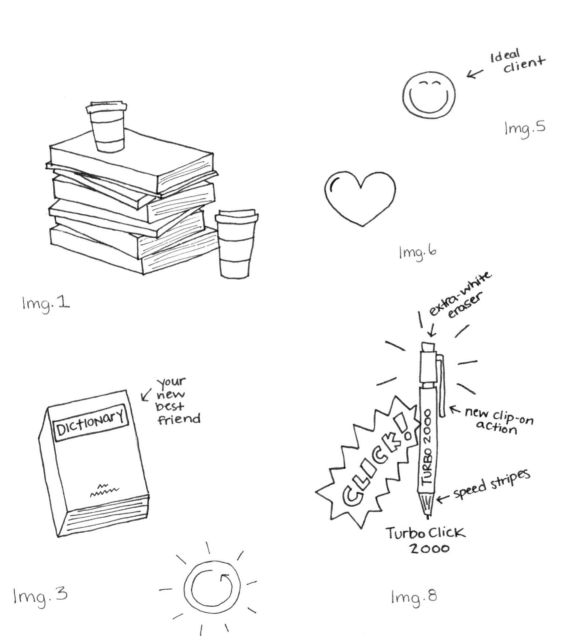

Img. 1

← Ideal
client

Img. 5

Img. 6

Linotype

I need music
everywhere I go

Img. 7

your
← new
best
friend

DICTIONARY

Img. 3

extra-white
eraser

CLICK!

← new clip-on
action

← speed stripes

Turbo Click
2000

Img. 8

Img

Flower
colorful
fragrant
vase
bud

EL
Flour Flour

bouquet
of flour
sacks

flour

bouquet

Img

Img. 9

582 DON'T FORCE YOURSELF TO DESIGN. Generally listen to music and drive around, usually ending up sitting in the aisle of a bookstore with a stack of design books. If I feel too forced to design, I get a mental block.

583 KEYWORDS + SKETCHES. I always start with a list of keywords and branch it off as far as I can, then I begin to sketch things out.

584 YOU HAVE TO RESEARCH! You can't expect to create smart design if you don't fully understand the topic. Knowing a product's origins, definitions, and history gives you a whole new set of keywords to play off of. For instance, with my Smart Design posters, I came to learn that SCAD (the acronym for the college) means a large quantity of something, as well as a type of fish. It was through that bit of information that the whole series was developed.

585 COLD CALL. The key is to keep the phone call under a minute—just be nice and ask if you can send along an e-mail with more information. The hard part is not pushing too hard. If you're friendly, they'll say yes out of courtesy at least, then may end up calling you back after all!

586 DON'T EVER SELL YOURSELF SHORT, AND PLEASE DON'T DO SPEC WORK! Try to work with people who don't underestimate the power of good design. If you have to convince a client that a logo cannot be made for under $250, then you're going to have a very tough relationship. We're providing them with a visual voice, which is crucial for the survival of their business. We're designers, not items for bid on eBay.

587 ALWAYS BE FRIENDLY. Design is about connecting with people on an emotional level. If you can't do that in everyday life, how can you expect to do that in your design?

588 ESCAPE IN MUSIC AND FILM. I find music to be vital to my creativity. I like to listen to things that go along with the feeling of the project I'm working on so I listen to a little of everything. I also love "escaping" in movies—it puts me in the mind of someone else and always seems to spark an idea for me.

589 GO OLD SCHOOL. I use pencil and paper—it works fine for me!

590 FOLLOW AND PRINT. Always follow your project. If my name is affixed to it, I have to make certain that everything is as it was intended. I've always enjoyed working with Brunner Printing in Memphis, Tennessee.

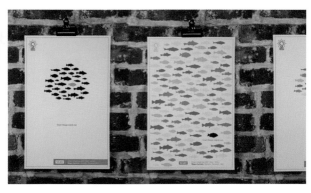

581
Have the big picture clear. In the words of King Solomon, "There's nothing new under the sun."
Designers have the challenge of expressing the same age-old ideas or products in a new and exciting way. There will always be fads, but they evolve into something new. A style may be re-visited, but it's going to have a twist on it the second time around. One thing that will never die out is good typography; from the *Book of Kells* to *GQ*, elegant and expressive type will always be prevalent.

Megan Cummins

www.megancummins.com

A young American designer, Megan received a BFA in Graphic Design at the Savannah College of Art and Design. Although a lover of the whole gamut of design, it's clear from her work how her heart lies with packaging; she's been creating fabulous Valentine's shoe boxes as early as second grade. Aside from design, she's a thrill-seeking sky and scuba diver (all for inspiration of course), and owns two crazy cats. Her vision of graphic design is close to scientific research, exploration, testing, and finding the right solution that produces the desired results. Vignelli's New York subway map that opened her eyes to the power of design, and she's been hooked ever since. One of her latest projects is the Smart Design Poster Series, a series of three posters designed for a Korean Design Expo explaining the idea visually.

Mostardesign

www.mostardesign.com

Olivier Gourvat originally worked as a graphic designer for various agencies, producing artwork, logotypes, corporate publicities, and print layouts. He later joined the team at Chronicle Editions to create image content, cover designs, illustrations, and maps for numerous books on the history of the twentieth century. Now, he owns and operates Mostardesign—a sort of "dematerialized" studio, in his words. He makes multi-disciplinary practice the base for all of his creative efforts, being active in print and digital design. His expertise also encompasses motion graphics and typeface creation for clients worldwide. Judging from his work, typography is the favorite playground, creating bold works and communication strategies that do not stop at image level, striving to deliver a product that can contain a message rather than just deliver it.

591 FOLLOW THE WRITTEN WORD. I recommend reading a great book written by John T. Drew and Sarah Meyer called *Colour Management for Packaging*. This excellent guide is a consolidated resource for the graphic designer who wants to create packages. This book covers both theoretical and practical packaging design, with many useful considerations.

592 4/4THS CONCENTRATION TECHNIQUE. Music helps me to be more creative and it's very hard for me to work without it. It's really like a second tool when I'm designing!

593 SMALL YELLOW IDEAS. My favorite organization tool is the Post-it™! Really a great idea in itself!

594 START TO PRINT, LEARN TO BROWSE. My favorite media is the web even if I began to work on print. I turned towards interactive design when I first got on the Internet. I remember being immediately fascinated by this new media and the broad creative possibilities it offered.

595 USE A LIMITED NUMBER OF FONTS. I use Avant Garde type in some projects, but my favorite font is Helvetica. I recommend installing a limited number of typefaces on your computer. Ten typefaces are really enough. This will give your future works more identity and more unity.

INTERNATIONALLY RENOWNED

Our work has been featured in books, magazines and e-zines such as News Today (USA), Netdiver Magazine (Montréal), Semi-Permanent Book (Australia), How design (USA), ROJO magazine (Spain), Root Magazine (Italy), Zupi Mag (Brazil), Praktica (France), Color Management Book (USA), New Web Pick (Japan), and more…

Books

Web design index - by Sigurd Buchberger (the Pepin press), November 2008
New Web Pick # 17 «Bruce Lee 32 35» - by New Web Pick, August 2008
Color Management for packaging «A comprehensive guide for graphic designers» - by John T. Drew and Sarah Mayer (Rotovision), p. 31, June 2008
Netadies 3 - by Zeixs (Feierabend unique books), May 2008
Pezo SÈVE - Ins beautiful states» By David Quiles Guilló (Sintonisan SL), p. 214, 215, 216, 217, 218, 219, May 2008
Typography - by Zeus (Feierabend unique books), p. 531, August 2007
Graphic Design - by Zeixs (Feierabend unique books), August 2007
Semi-Permanent book 2007 (Design: is Kinky FTY Ltd), p. 160, February 2007
8 th International Poster Triennel catalog, p 130, August 2006
Zupi Magazine #1 - By Allan Sonscher, p.60, May 2006

Exhibitions

8 th International Poster Triennial in in Museum of Modern Art of Toyama - IPT 2006 Uapana

Third ICTVC International Conferences on Typography and Visual Communication (Greece)

4 th Istanbul International Animation Festival (Turkey)

ROJO TV Spain

Interview

Technohart. «Le Web design transcends la fabrication de l'image» p. 56, 33, April 2008

Web Design International Festival, November 2007

596 PLUG-INS, SCHMPLUG-INS. I recommend you to forget about every plug-in installed in your computer. Photoshop plug-ins limit creativity and should be forbidden! Also, I believe they give your creations a certain feeling of déjà vu.

597 SKETCH!

598 PROMOTE EACH AND EVERY PROJECT. Generally I promote each project made by the studio with a photo. Try to find the best way to promote each work through a beautiful photo for the main page of your website or for an insert in the next version of your portfolio! For one project I staged a high resolution visual adding our very own Mostardesign cocktail to help display the works created (business card, booklets, visual identity, etc.). The official recipe is available on our website.

599 REGARDING PORTFOLIOS. My philosophy is to fully dematerialize self-promotion material. I always have a light version of my portfolio in PDF format in order to make it easily e-mailable.

600 HAVE A TRADEMARK COLOR COMBO. An olive green, a light blue, and a classic black—these three colors are the identity of the studio. I have also created a section on my web site with combinations for each project to have as a kind of bank of combinations to refer to.

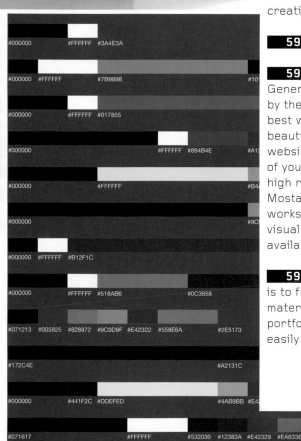

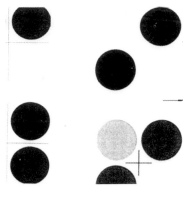

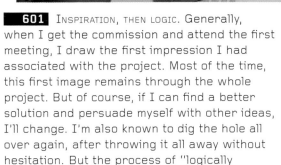

601 INSPIRATION, THEN LOGIC. Generally, when I get the commission and attend the first meeting, I draw the first impression I had associated with the project. Most of the time, this first image remains through the whole project. But of course, if I can find a better solution and persuade myself with other ideas, I'll change. I'm also known to dig the hole all over again, after throwing it all away without hesitation. But the process of "logically persuading myself" is very important.

602 WORDS, THEN SKETCHES. Brainstorming with keywords can help some part, but this is only for supporting ideas in your brain and providing descriptions for your commissioners. Drawing and sketching by hand is best.

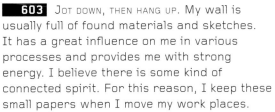

603 JOT DOWN, THEN HANG UP. My wall is usually full of found materials and sketches. It has a great influence on me in various processes and provides me with strong energy. I believe there is some kind of connected spirit. For this reason, I keep these small papers when I move my work places.

604 SHARE, THEN COLLABORATE. Clients are difficult to get and even more difficult to pick. As an independent designer now, I work with some clients who are interested in my work, they usually figure as people who share common interests with me. There is no specific way to find this out at first. But naturally, people can notice someone who has connection with them, like an impression.

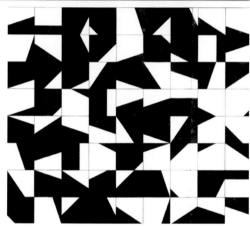

605
Absorb, then create. I try to absorb as much as possible around myself. That can be a landscape, a small flyer on the street, a junky magazine, or even a good meal. Anything can be! Not just something that we can refer to as a standard "source of creation." Creativity feels like a strange word for me, that forces me to make something. But of course, all of these sources build up my personality and way of attitude thus affecting my work and design process.

606 Poised, then smiley. I have to say you have to be friendly. But in certain occasions, being serious can be a friendly way, and vice versa.

607 Choose media, choose strategies. Different media have different strategies of getting through to people. In most cases, I work on printed matters and I love the paper-based media. I studied product design before, so I'm also familiar with 3D media and textile materials. But I'm not so attracted to web-based digital media, it's such a flat and cold way of communication.

608 Think, then fold. Grid systems are very important in design, but you must not start with a rigid grid structure. It creates strong principles in design detail, but it prevents you from seeing the wider picture. Draw the sketch and fold the paper by hand.

609 Local, yet global. It is essential to think about what you are doing as an independent designer. Unlike artists, designers are needed to follow directions. But the brief shouldn't prevent you from losing your own language and expressing who you are and what you want to say to the world. You have to be aware of your influences and interaction with the public. Even if this cannot change the world, every small activity is significant in itself.

610 Keys, then words. Thin paper, black and white, paper cutting, stickers, craft-paper, open binding, type press, A0 size poster, photocopy, silk-screen, tape, stationery shop, cold glue, archive, wall graphic, label, map, supermarket, black square, red line, color paper, wallpaper, rainbow, folding-paper tool, minimal, accident, 10mm square note, A3 printer, street signs, blue wall, inventing tools, drum and bass, acrylic plate.

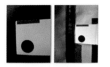

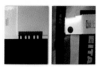

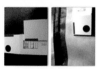

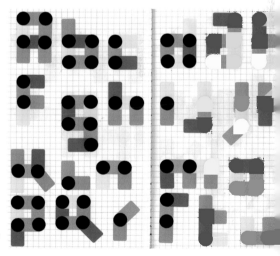

Na Kim

www.ynkim.com

Na Kim studied Product Design at the Korea Advanced Institute of Science and Technology and graphic design at Hongik University. Upon finishing her studies, she went on to Werkplaats Typografie in Arnhem in 2006. She was selected as the Young Design Leader in 2008 gaining publication in *Wallpaper** magazine. She organized the exhibitions WT at Neon in Lyon in 2007 and Starting from Zero in Seoul. The latter event received broad press coverage, such as a mention in *Grafik*. Now she lives and works in Amsterdam, in collaboration with many artists and cultural clients, such as, Phaidon, bak, Tumult, Océ, and DF&DC. Occasionally she'll work on self-initiated projects, like *umool umool* magazine. She was invited as a guest lecturer at the Gerrit Rietveld Academie, Hongik University, and Kyewon Art College.

Nate Yates

www.nateyates.com

Born and raised in San Diego, California, Nate Yates grew up surrounded by the Mexican culture. He lived in a run-down neighborhood, but is very glad that he did, learning much more about life there than he would have by living in the quiet suburbs. His art teacher was the first person who introduced him to graphic design in his senior year. Nate states: "Being a practical lady, she had no delusions of grandeur for me, so she gave it to me straight—'Nate, don't try to be some starving artist, you should be a graphic designer.'" He never had a desire to do anything else since, and continued his education at San Diego State and City College to create his portfolio. In 2004, he was awarded first place in the AIGA San Diego Student Portfolio Review.

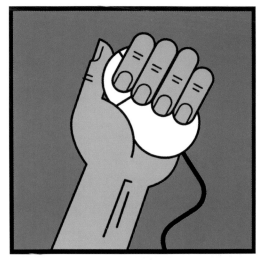

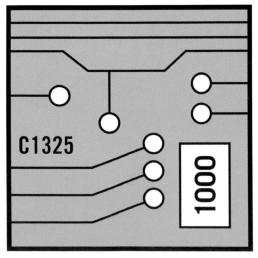

611 BE PASSIONATE.

612 DON'T GET COCKY.

613 USE THE LATEST TECHNOLOGY.

614 COLLABORATE.

615 DO INSPIRATIONAL ACTIVITIES.

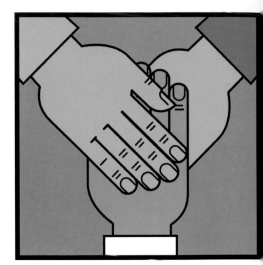

616 Learn different mediums.

617 Get idea suggestions.

618 Don't design for awards.

619 Be confident.

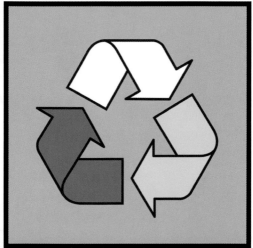

620
Reinvent yourself.

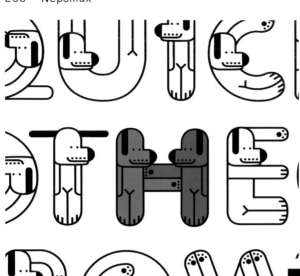

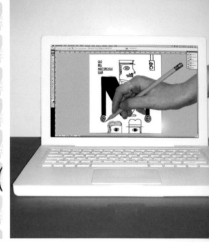

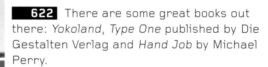

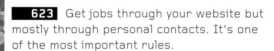

621 Graphic design is about opening your eyes towards your environment and adapting what you see to your work. In addition, we find design books and design blogs very inspiring.

622 There are some great books out there: *Yokoland*, *Type One* published by Die Gestalten Verlag and *Hand Job* by Michael Perry.

623 Get jobs through your website but mostly through personal contacts. It's one of the most important rules.

624 Clients should know your style before getting in touch. In that way, they know what they can expect.

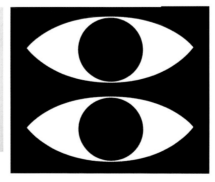

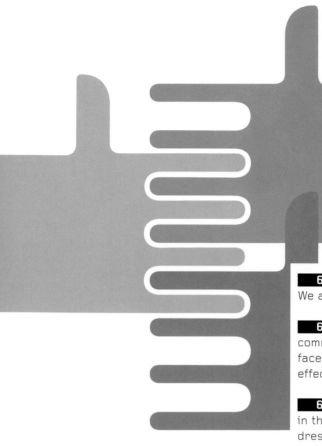

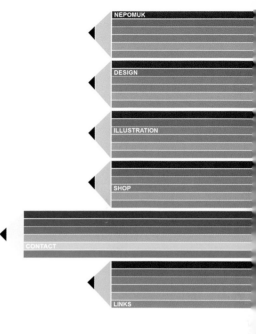

625 Be serious to appear trustworthy. We are all innately friendly.

626 Without e-mail and phone you can't communicate today, can you? But talking face-to-face is the most personal and effective.

627 It's important to feel comfortable in the clothes we wear. There is no special dress code. And it is not always black. It could be chic as well as casual, just natural.

628 We have recently discovered this font: Berlin Park by Daniel Dolz.

629 Chemistry between people is key.

630
Create your work in a space that ranges from creative chaos to purism.

Nepomuk

www.nepomukworld.com

A studio created by Sven Neitzel, Doris Freigofas and Daniel Dolz, three graphic designers from Berlin, born in the former GDR in the early 80s. Nepomuk is a fictive name for a figure that is open to your imagination. The trio met during their studies at the Universität der Künste Berlin, UdK (Berlin University of the Arts) and felt a sort of creative connection. They are interested both in graphic design and in illustration and always try to create work that combines the fortes of both disciplines. Usually drawing inspiration out of the pulsating city that surrounds them, as well as the silence and solitude of nature. Nepomuk believes that it's important to find a balance, to not get lost in the big stream and to find one's own creativity. Lately they issued *Urban Alphabet*, a new book consisting of an edition of 350 offset prints.

Nicolas Thiebault-Pikor

www.nicolasthiebaultpikor.fr

After having graduated from the École des Beaux-Arts de Rennes and the Institut universitaire de technologie de Reims and having followed other paths in other times, Nicolas Thiebault-Pikor claims to be still moving through the dark. Nevertheless, his graphic preoccupations and commitments encouraged him to follow one post-graduation year on typography at the École Supérieure d'Art et Design d'Amiens. Despite the rain, he keeps exploring optical typography, constantly wondering about pictures, white, black, consumer society, masses, geometry, camouflage, haze, the universe, and everything.

His latest project is a reflection on the letter and how it hides in its surroundings. Putting some white in the letter and some black on the page, here are the final points. By use of the moiré effect and other optical effects, he aims to confuse—and amaze—the beholder.

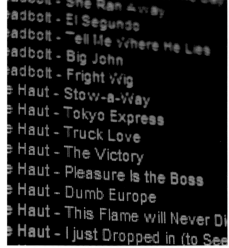

631 The concept of an idea is really vague: you can imagine that they float on the surface of the world and that you can go and take them, use them, mix them, and put them back where they come from. Which allows for a "general emulsion" in which every man, every potential creator owns a global source of knowledge that he is using and to which he is giving as well. This makes the world go round. In theory, everything can give you an idea. You might just need to go down the street and buy some bread or a few beers and find out. The first idea is usually the right one, you just need to use it the right way.

632 A small scribbling and a few keywords allow to set the first idea. The human and visual knowledge will do the rest. The word "knowledge" is a bit strong, curiosity and willingness to learn would be more appropriate.

633 Watch a lot of movies, series, and cartoons. I look at the world revolving around me, I take walks quite often and listen to music most of the time. We can't really say that it helps create but it might give me some ideas and allow me to evolve (as a human being as well as a designer).
I don't do sports, it's too tiring.

634 My professor, Gerard Paris-Clavel, said during a workshop: "Don't refer to design books because it limits your imagination."

635 I love fonts that have something to say (for example, J. Barnbrook's Bastard). I really like ligatures of Lubalin's Avant Garde, but mostly because it's in fashion. I hate Comic Sans MS, but mostly because it's fashionable to hate it. To tell you the truth, I have a wonderful t-shirt made with Comic Sans MS, but nothing with Avant Garde.

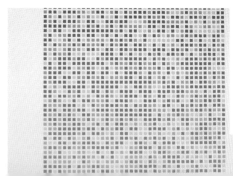

636 If you meet a new person every week, it will allow you to meet new people who will in turn allow you to meet their contacts, and so on. It's a good way of building a random but totally human network. You shouldn't limit yourself to a designer's world revolving on itself.

637 When you work you shouldn't forget hierarchy. But the most important thing is to stay true to yourself.

638 I personally developed a small Flash application that picks out three random colors. Many combinations pass in front of my eyes and when I'm happy with one, I'll use it.

639 Whatever the circumstances, do not give anything up for a client if it means doing something you don't want to. Never abandon your own ideas and stay true to yourself— and don't listen to me!

640 As long as you are aware of the basis of Tschichold, everything seems possible. I never follow a grid or anything when I work. You can see that I follow a lot of graphic curiosities and own instincts in my work. A mistake is something to consider in the overall project, although you need to know why you keep it, and why it's interesting.

641 Less is more.

642 Less isn't more.

643 More is less.

644 More isn't less.

645 A picture is worth a thousand words.

646 A picture isn't worth a thousand words.

647 A word is worth a thousand pictures.

648 A word isn't worth a thousand pictures.

649 The abovementioned is true.

650 The abovementioned isn't true.

Niels "Shoe" Meulman
www.nielsshoemeulman.com

Born and raised in Amsterdam, Niels Meulman's initial recognition came as "Shoe" within local and international graffiti culture. This evolved into a business for decorative lettering when he was eighteen. Eager to learn more, Meulman became apprentice to Dutch graphic design master Anthon Beeke to learn the trade. Throughout the 90s Meulman ran his own design company Caulfield & Tensing, before joining advertising agency BBDO as senior art director. In recent years, he has been working as a creative director for MTV Europe but mostly freelances under his own name: Niels "Shoe" Meulman and specializes in typographic design. His designs and artwork are part of the permanent collection of the Stedelijk Museum Amsterdam and the San Francisco MOMA.

Pam&Jenny
www.pametjenny.be

Nathalie Pollet has been a graphic designer since 1992. After finishing her studies, she started a career as a freelance designer for record companies and concert halls in Brussels. She co-founded the Designlab studio in 1998 where she was creative director and studio manager for 11 years.

Most of her clients come from the cultural sector in Belgium and France: Bureau d'architecture V+ (Bruxelles), CIVA—Centre International pour la Ville, l'Architecture et le Paysage (Bruxelles), Lille3000 (Lille). Projects are mainly in the areas of identities for museums and festivals,

communication for cultural centers, art galleries, exhibits, dance companies, art and architecture magazines, and lately signage. In the beginning of 2009, she started a new studio named Pam&Jenny: new name, same spirit, lighter structure.

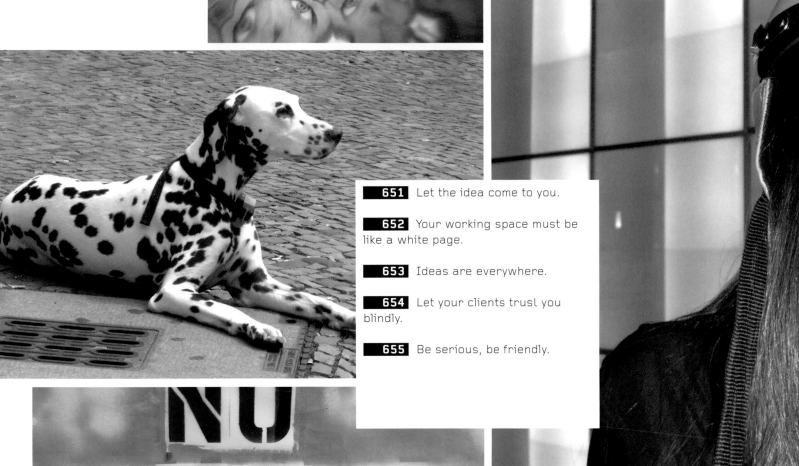

651 Let the idea come to you.

652 Your working space must be like a white page.

653 Ideas are everywhere.

654 Let your clients trusl you blindly.

655 Be serious, be friendly.

656 White and black. Timeless color combination.

657 Every detail counts.

658 Organize your timelines. Or, work late.

659 Always try something else.

660
Don't trust a badly-dressed designer.

661 RESPECT THE ORIGIN OF THE IDEA. I mostly work on commercial typefaces, so ideas and decisions taken are market-driven. This means I have to watch out for trends coming from selected directions such as music, fashion, visual arts, technology. A new design reflects these trends as well as the surrounding environment i.e. the various structural shapes such as architectural buildings, industrial objects, and even just plain natural structures. The idea behind Centro Pro (an award winning font that Parachute® designed) was to combine modern square forms with traditional shapes in such a way as not to distract legibility. The serifs would have to reflect the simplicity of a contemporary building. Furthermore, extreme care was taken so that the pronounced triangular cuts were properly connected and balanced with round forms to avoid creating a strange-looking typeface. Finally, it was decided to support all European scripts—Latin, Greek, and Cyrillic—in order to satisfy a growing demand among pan-European companies and institutions for such typefaces.

662 RESEARCH THOROUGHLY. It always helps to look back to what the masters of the trade have done. Some characteristics of Centro Pro serif were modeled after W.A. Dwiggins's experiments with type. The angular slanted serifs of Centro Pro, in letters like "n," "p," "r," etc., while they foster a distinct identity at display sizes, they tend to look like curves at small sizes. Other characteristics such as the abrupt cut at the joints were influenced by Galfra, a typeface designed in 1975 by Ladislas Mandel for the Italian phone directory. These cuts add certain flair to Centro Pro serif especially at display sizes, but they are functional as well, since at small sizes, while they disappear into rounded curves, they compensate for over-inking.

663 DRAFTING THE IDEA. In most cases the idea is drafted initially on a piece of paper, a rough sketch of several characters with as many characteristics as I can fit on paper. Then I create a second, more elaborate sketch of three basic characters such as "a," "n," and "o." These are the three letters I always design first since they contain many of the characteristics as I need as a guide for the design of other characters. Then everything is finalized in FontLab. There are also a few instances (particularly for text typefaces, which follow certain rules and consist of well-defined forms) that a design may start right on the computer by playing around with one of my older designs.

664 BOOKS. Of all, there are four books on typography which I consider a total must, as each one complements the other: *American Metal Typefaces of the 20th Century* by Mac McGrew, *Elements of Typographic Style* by Robert Bringhurst, *Letters of Credit* by Walter Tracy, *Writing & Illuminating & Lettering* by Edward Johnston.

665 PAY ATTENTION TO DETAIL. This is one of your characteristics that set you apart from the crowd. Things like spacing or kerning of characters as well as the proper position or shape of accents, are very important for a demanding customer. In Centro Pro, the main concern right from the beginning was not only the shape of the characters but the rhythm of text as well. If letters are not properly spaced, the text will be hard to read. First, the basic spacing (sidebearing adjustment) for capitals "H" and "O" as well as lowercase "n" and "o" was set. Then, for every new character created, the sidebearings were adjusted based on the similarities of its straight or round strokes to the letters used as reference. Proper positioning of accents was also double-checked and adjusted.

Falcon *Falcon 1*

a d e f g r *Experimen*

parole *Galfra 19*

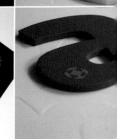

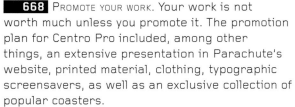

667 GIVE MORE THAN EXPECTED. Add extra value to your product without raising the price. Every font in the Centro Pro series was completed with 270 copyright-free symbols, some of which have been proposed by several international organizations for packaging, public areas, environment, transportation, computers, and fabric care. These are quite useful and handy to designers involved with branding, packaging, and products with international appeal.

668 PROMOTE YOUR WORK. Your work is not worth much unless you promote it. The promotion plan for Centro Pro included, among other things, an extensive presentation in Parachute's website, printed material, clothing, typographic screensavers, as well as an exclusive collection of popular coasters.

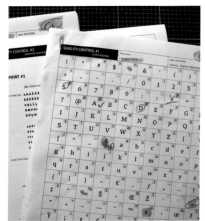

669 WORK SCHEDULE. Don't work on the same project more than a few days in a row. I have the tendency to get stuck in minor details trying to perfect things, so I find it more productive to just drop it, work for a while on a different project, and later come back with a clear head to find the solution.

666
ALWAYS DELIVER WHAT YOU PROMISE.
Minimize problems by passing your design through extensive quality control. The Centro Pro series supports more than 100 languages and each font contains an enormous number of glyphs. This situation may easily get out of hand as some glyphs could be placed mistakenly in the wrong position. In order to overcome such problems, we devised a quality control method—i.e. two sets of tables which we use to check the proper position of glyphs as well as OT features.

670 DEFY RULES. This is a motto that always reminds me of what I want to do and not necessarily what I do.

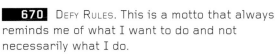

Parachute®

www.parachute.gr

Panos Vassiliou is the mastermind behind Parachute. Two years after his graduation from the University of Toronto, where he studied Applied Science and Engineering, he pursued a teaching career at George Brown College in Toronto. He has been Creative Director for the Canadian design firm AdHaus and publisher of *DNA*‹ magazine. He has been designing typefaces since 1993 and commercial fonts as well as commissions from major companies. After moving to Greece, he started Parachute® in 1999 setting the base for a typeface library that reflected the works of some of the best contemporary Greek designers, as well as type-obsessed creatives. He received a design award for his typeface Archive at the EBGE Awards 2004. In 2008, he won another major international award at the European Design Awards, for the typeface superfamilies Centro Pro.

Patrick Fry

www.patrickfry.co.uk

A freelance designer from London. Since graduating from the London College of Communication, Patrick Fry has worked across a variety of mediums such as stop motion animation, hand-drawn illustration, typography, and corporate identities. He is currently working from his studio in Hackney on a number of commercial and self-initiated projects. Some of his projects include: *Unordinary People* (design and art direction of a book celebrating 50 years of PYMCA photographs which was later recreated as an exhibition at The Royal Albert Hall), Beardyman (a variety of visuals for champion beat boxer Beardyman; each piece focuses on Beardyman's mischevious and highly adaptable qualities), and *Tested Negative* (a book for GMFA, advising gay men on how to stay negative).

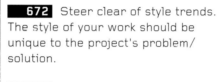

671 Communication should always come first.

672 Steer clear of style trends. The style of your work should be unique to the project's problem/ solution.

673 Don't settle for the easy processes, sometimes the harder route will create a more unique solution.

674 Look for inspiration in strange places, not just in your own industry.

EXPERIMENTAL ADVANCED SUPERCONDUCTING TOKAMAK

675 Learn about everything. The more you know, the more likely you will find that great solution.

676 Get away from your computer. Make every project contain something that a program cannot create alone.

677 Make budget problems into design solutions. Work with your budget not against it.

678 Collaborate as much as possible. Two brains are always better than one.

679 Always keep a personal project running, for all those great ideas that never see the light of day.

Lucy Barber
PR Manager

71 St John St
London EC1M 4NJ
www.thinkespionage.com

Phone +44 (0)20 7251 8448
Mobile +44 (0)7841 132 612
Email lucy@thinkespionage.com

680
Enjoy your accidents and make them part of the work.

681 WORDS AND IDEAS. I've found that talking about the idea helps, even if the person you're talking to has no understanding of the subject matter or isn't interested. It's incredible how different ideas become once they're audible and how other elements come to light as you explain your concept. I used to get quite precious about my initial ideas and subsequently didn't let them evolve. I would have a preconceived solution in my head and found I was reluctant to deviate from that. In those circumstances I didn't produce a single piece of work that I was proud of. Use sketchbooks, if possible, but any type of printed record is good. I find it's very helpful to take screen shots of the document as you make changes then print them out as thumbnails. Things look remarkably different when they're printed out, it also gives you an excellent account of how the project has progressed and the different directions it's taken. I tend to take things too far and have been advised countless times by people in the studio to take it back a stage or two. This wouldn't have been possible if the iterations had stayed on my computer.

682 RESEARCH FOR A BRIEF. There are many ways of researching for a brief. If it's an identity project you're probably going to be talking to the people within the company, finding out what their viewpoint is and how they think the company should be perceived. If it's print or web, it's always a good idea to have a look at contemporary solutions to similar projects, in my opinion anyway, to see what is the most effective way of solving a given problem and why that method works. From there you may decide to discard all your research and take a different road but I find it's good to have a grasp on what is successful and why.

683 SMASHING BOOK. *Sorry Trees,* Vince Frost.

684 CLIENTS BRING CLIENTS. That's useless advice if you currently haven't got any clients but it is the case. Doing things for friends can be good, self initiated work is often a good bet but just make sure you give yourself a brief or parameters from the outset and stick to them. It's far too easy to let a project trail off when you're the client and ultimately you just end up getting bored with it.

685 WORKING WITH YOU IS GREAT. Open-minded clients are wonderful; though they need to be decisive too. I can't emphasize enough how important it is to listen to them during your elementary meetings. If they feel their ideas are being valued and taken on board you're far more likely to have your own ideas met in a similar way. The relationship works both ways and it's very important to grasp that before meeting any client.

Visual
Commu-
nication

Dublin Bay
Architecture
Symposium

2008

10.08

686 FACE TO FACE, EYE TO EYE. It's not so much a single tool, all are good in different situations; meeting face to face is still number one; next to that, the phone and e-mail.

687 GRIDS ARE PRETENTIOUS. It will save you an obscene amount of time and ensure your friends who aren't designers think you're pretentious. In all honesty, though, a grid is a really great idea, like every other rule they don't have to be obeyed absolutely but they provide a fantastic basis especially if you're doing a project with a number of pages.

688 SOULLESS COLORS. Because I have no soul, I love silver (Pantone 877) on black, especially if it's dense information or has some infographic quality. I also did a book recently replacing magenta and yellow with day glow inks (fluorescent colors). It turned out really nice and I've been suggesting it to clients ever since. Doesn't really suit most briefs though.

689 PRESENT YOUR WORK THROUGH DIFFERENT MEDIA. It's really all of the above. A website is very handy for people to look at it at their leisure, a PDF file is a great idea to send out to selected studios, and a print portfolio is a necessity if you're going for interviews. Just be ready and able to talk about your work in any of the above.

690 ORDER IT, BREAK IT, DISMANTLE IT. I like to apply order first; my work is nearly always too austere and regimented a week or two before it goes to print. I like to work it up so that it functions properly, satisfies all reason, then I like to break it. Over print, offset or otherwise. It's only after I've designed it to death that I begin to un-design it again. I've noticed myself do that on most projects I've worked on. The more successful ones are the ones that I've had more time to dismantle.

Patrick Mullen

www.patrickmullendesign.com

There are many things to learn about Patrick when he describes his "initiation" to art and design: "We were always drawing and painting as kids, my brother was a natural and so I took a backseat somewhere before my teens and shelved my creativity for a little while." He went on to study at the Institute of Art Design and Technology, Dun Laoghaire, Ireland. Thanks to two tutors, he ended up falling in love with design and went on to graduate in 2008 top of the class with first class honors. His dad's influence and his own interest in architecture began to manifest itself in his final year. Most notably though, much of his work has a certain architectural structure to it, the use of thin lines and the reasonably austere nature and certainly is a direct result of staring at and coloring-in architectural drawings from a very young age.

Pedro Vilas-Boas

www.vilaz.tv

Conceived by Antonio and Carmelinda in the first half of the 80s, Pedro Vilas-Boas, a.k.a. Vilaz, is a multi-disciplinary designer from Pavia, Portugal. During his youth, he formed as a student a love of cars (which he drove for the first time at age eight) and the broad color palette of his native Alentejo. He studied Communication Design at Universidade do Algarve, then he moved to Lisbon were he went on to gain years of industry experience at ByCom and Fullsix. Those experiences respectivley taught him how to "think design" and how to "think digital design." He currently divides his time between Lisbon and Paris. He has a special taste for the experimental and always applies it in commercial works. His work is characterized by the use of vibrant colors and a controlled chaos.

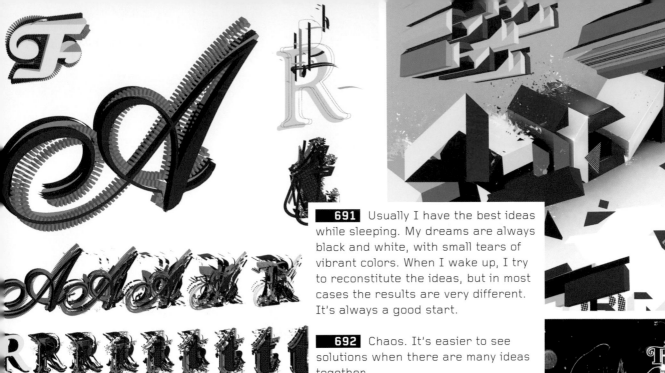

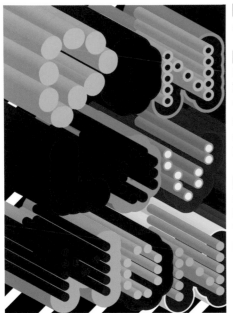

691 Usually I have the best ideas while sleeping. My dreams are always black and white, with small tears of vibrant colors. When I wake up, I try to reconstitute the ideas, but in most cases the results are very different. It's always a good start.

692 Chaos. It's easier to see solutions when there are many ideas together.

693 Do not be afraid of the absurd when the briefing allows it.

694 Music can be a great ally to build (or destroy). Sometimes I let myself be absorbed by the music while trying to illustrate the beats graphically, the rhythms, and the sounds mixing. Music can sometimes be a great input to our creativity.

695 Sometimes, not being completely in control of software will help you to get unforeseen results. When possible, experimentation can be a good creative source.

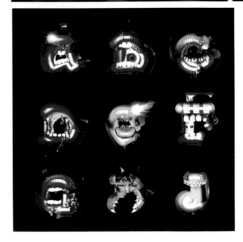

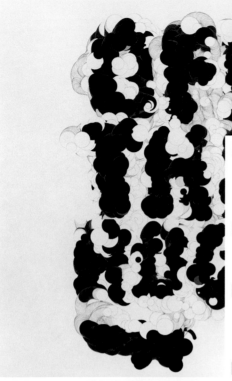

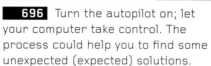

696 Turn the autopilot on; let your computer take control. The process could help you to find some unexpected (expected) solutions.

697 A good way to find new shapes is deconstructing some of our work.

698 When I have doubts about colors, I take a picture of different and nicely colored objects and take my pick.

699 Ask the opinion of someone who you consider a better designer. That way, you'll always have a safe boat. It's important to have an honest opinion of others, and it's very important to recognize, listen, and accept critiques.

700
I like to seek inspiration in nostalgia.
When I was a child, I loved the feeling of receiving candy, the wrap paper, the attractive colors, their happiness, more than the way they tasted.
I try to inspire myself with small memories and tiny, happy moments I experienced.

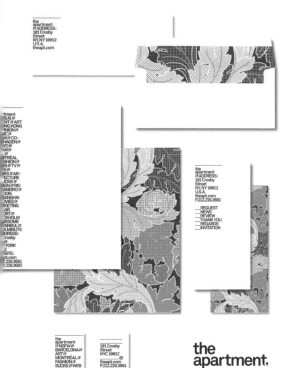

701 Most ideas come from a desire to express a particular emotion or concept. This is especially true of my information visualization work where in addition to expressing a complex concept or set of emotions, there is also a story to tell. In my A_B project, for example, I've tried to create an informational visualization piece that revolves around complex personal and collective notions of national identity and how identity fits into global contributions to peace and terror.

702 I only ever use words to sketch an idea. I find visual sketching much too deterministic and directional--I much more prefer generalized words and terms that allow my imagination to be piqued and specifics to be determined without visuals to be set and therefore restricted.

703 Music: Littl'ans, Foals, The Big Pink, Underground Resistance, The Veils, Arvo Part. Art: Jan van Munster, Damien Hirst, Troika, Scott King. Literature: *The Guardian*, Baudelaire, *Les Chants de Maldoror*, anything by Robert Fisk. Cinema: *If...*, *Begotten*, *Showgirls*.

704 The mind is much more elastic when the body is forced to use different senses.

705 Creatives who don't do research are arrogant fools and rarely have anything of value to say. Research can come from any source—so long as it is reliable and fills in the blanks of knowledge.

THE RIGHT TO FREE ASSEM-BLY & ASSOCI-ATION

706
Don't hate. Life is too short for hate.

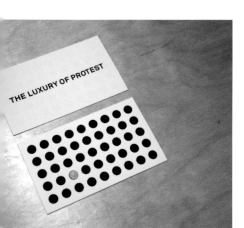

THE LUXURY OF PROTEST

love will tear us apart again.

love will tear us apart again.

707 The day before a deadline, I panic enough to finally finish the project.

708 Work everywhere and at anytime—while waiting in line, on the toilet, at the dentist getting a root canal, and most definitely in the throws of physical ecstasy.

709 Try this font: Akkurat.

710 Try this finish: GFSmith Plasma Polycoat Glass Clear Plastic. Absolutely amazing for silk-screening.

N-OPoIS

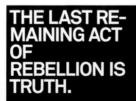

THE LAST RE-MAINING ACT OF REBELLION IS TRUTH.

the apartment.

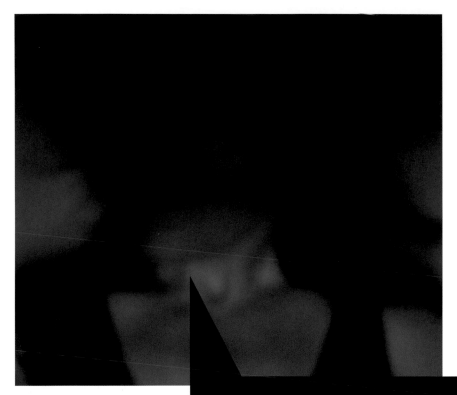

Peter Crnokrak

www.theluxuryofprotest.com

Born Peter Crnokrak in Croatia. Emigrated to Windsor, Canada at the age of two. Discovered The Smiths when he was 15. Danced to Detroit Techno in Detroit 1988. Moved to London, Canada to study Medicine, then to Montreal to complete a doctorate in evolutionary genetics. Deejayed right before Jeff Mills at New Year's party in Montreal in 1999. Moved to Toronto to start a post-doctoral fellowship but became crushingly bored with life. Back to Montreal 2002 for two years of art college and glorious 18-hour work days. Graduated in 2004 and found the graphic design practice ± design. Moved to NYC in 2006 to work in the apartment and flirt with sweet girls, then to London, UK in fall 2007. Dropped the ± moniker and founded The Luxury of Protest.

Pied De Mouche

www.pieddemouche.fr

Pied De Mouche is a graphic design practice based in Paris. Founded and run by Alice Déchelette, Géraldine Roussel and Tom Bücher. The three met during the course of their studies in École Supérieure de Design, d'Art Graphique et d'Architecture Intérieure in Penninghen. They all share the same passion for contemporary art, but express it in different ways: by illustration, layouts, or typography. Pied De Mouche tries to blend these different disciplines to fulfill the client's brief. Apart from client work, they also set time aside for personal projects to explore other directions. This is fundamental to keep their studio practice always innovative, as shown in their projects in poster design like Théâtre La Bruyère, Rock'n roll, Le temps, Drogues Info Service, L'art d'en faire trop.

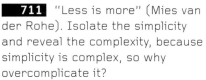

711 "Less is more" (Mies van der Rohe). Isolate the simplicity and reveal the complexity, because simplicity is complex, so why overcomplicate it?

712 These words encapsulate our approach to design: "Controlled disorder is creative." The independence of the idea allows the creative work a life of its own.

713 You must have faith in your project because you're the only one to fully understand it until it's completed.

714 Create a font for each project so that every project has its own identity.

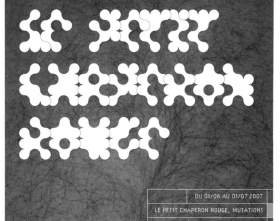

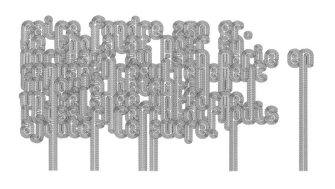

MON MARI EST
UN HOMME
MERVEILLEUX
J'AI DEUX ENFANTS
EXTRAORDINAIRES
NOUS AVONS
DES AMIS
FORMIDABLES
JE NE DORS PLUS
SANS CALMANT
TOUT VA TRES BIEN

716 "Never create like others before you" (Kurt Schwitters). "Because it's useless" (us).

717 You must have a real vision, your own vision, like an artist or a filmmaker has his own language. However, you have to adapt your vision to your client.

718 Ideas come any time, therefore you must always have a pencil on you, although sometimes you won't write anything. And if you remember an idea one week later, then you'll know it was a really good idea. Sometimes chance is better than human rationality.

719 We don't find, we search.

720 Don't take this advice literally.

715
The eventual form is inherent in the initial concept. Because every idea is a response to a question, and the question is apparent in the designer's solution.

CACOPHONIE

AL-
PHA-
BET

FROST NIXON

— BY PETER MORGAN —

PLAZM
28

721 Be obsessive.

722 Be true to yourself. Do what you love.

723 Try new things. Work without a safety net.

724 Work with people you haven't worked with before.

725 Don't over-present. Never show something you can't live with. Always keep something in your back pocket.

CREATING MORE WORLD

FROM BROOKLYN STREETS TO COMPUTERS EVERYWHERE.

LUCK

this way to nikebeautiful

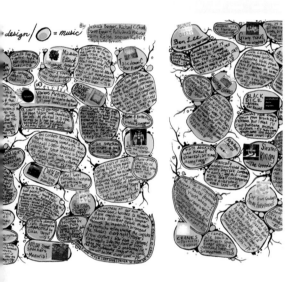

726 Don't under-present. Work up to the last second. What are you missing?

727 Give back. Mentor.

728 Use design for good. It is through design that messages reach people most effectively. Designers are trained in methods of mass communication and propaganda—we have a vast potential as agents for social change. I believe design can change the world.

729 Seek first to understand, then to be understood.

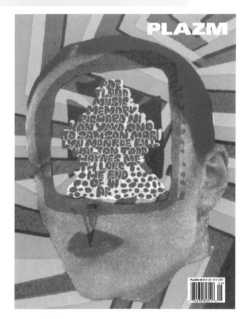

730
It's an analog world.

Plazm
www.plazm.com

Joshua Berger is founder and creative director of Plazm, a design firm serving commercial clients and social causes. He is also the publisher of *Plazm Magazine*. Berger's clients, include Nike, Lucasfilm, MTV, Jantzen Swimwear, Wieden+Kennedy, TBWA/Chiat Day, and the Portland Institute for Contemporary Art, among others. Plazm has been listed by *ID* magazine as one of the most influential firms in the world and received the Creative Resistance Award from Adbusters. The studio's depth of experience with editorial design is showcased in the Plazm-authored *XXX: The Power of Sex in Contemporary Design* and other books. The complete catalog of *Plazm Magazine* resides in the permanent collections of the Denver Art Museum and the San Francisco Museum of Modern Art.

Proekt

www.proekt.co.uk

It turns out to be that there are no positions in Proekt, but there are people. They have talent and abilities and through planned out thought everyone finds his or her own place in the studio. So designers can be a copywriters, copywriters can occasionally be illustrators, and illustrators can turn into designers. Every person works in the field where he or she can obtain interesting and effective results. Creative director Roman Krikheli believes that this is the way of attaining perfection. It goes without saying that there is some routine in such kind of work. Habit is an integral part of the process, being the price for evolution in any field of activity. An example of their workflow is their Parad boutique rebranding, where collective effort brought about a logo designed as a woman's lips—the origin of passion and wisdom.

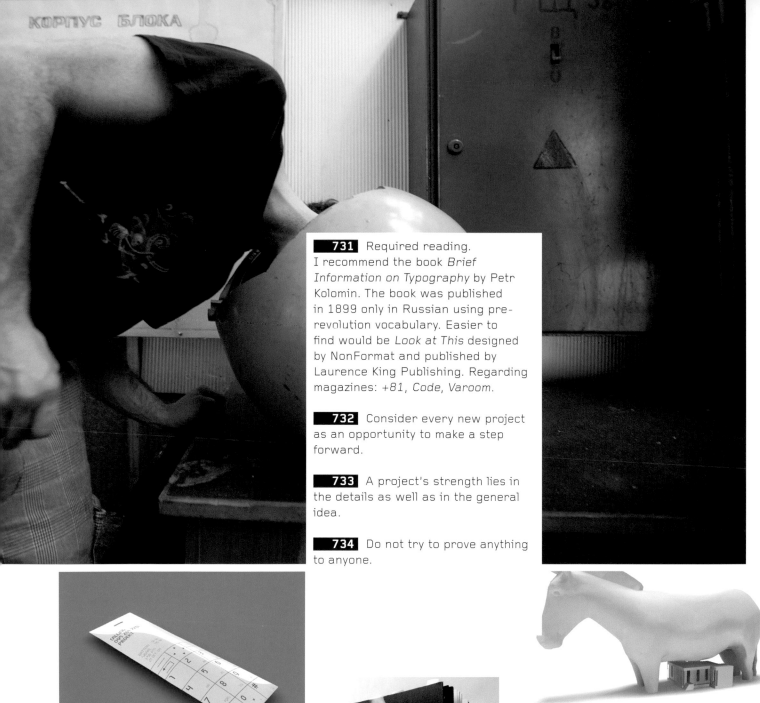

731 Required reading. I recommend the book *Brief Information on Typography* by Petr Kolomin. The book was published in 1899 only in Russian using pre-revolution vocabulary. Easier to find would be *Look at This* designed by NonFormat and published by Laurence King Publishing. Regarding magazines: *+81*, *Code*, *Varoom*.

732 Consider every new project as an opportunity to make a step forward.

733 A project's strength lies in the details as well as in the general idea.

734 Do not try to prove anything to anyone.

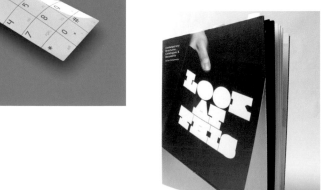

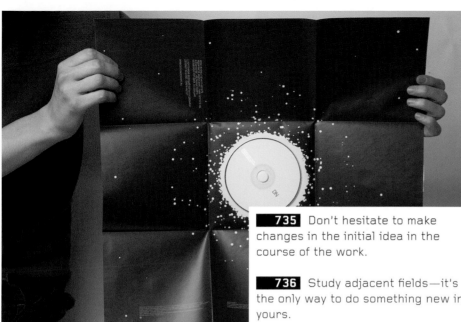

735 Don't hesitate to make changes in the initial idea in the course of the work.

736 Study adjacent fields—it's the only way to do something new in yours.

737 Never use the same idea twice.

738 Do not argue, discuss.

739 Remember, you can succeed in any field, if you have a key to the essence of the process.

740
Good design is always sweat and blood.

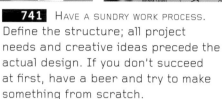

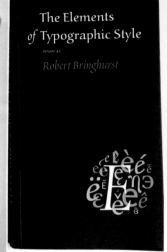

741 HAVE A SUNDRY WORK PROCESS. Define the structure; all project needs and creative ideas precede the actual design. If you don't succeed at first, have a beer and try to make something from scratch.

742 NEVER LEAVE THE HOUSE WITHOUT A SKETCHBOOK. I like plain paper and a pencil and the speed at which I can change and note things on paper. I recommend to all the designers never to forget how to use pencil and paper. Those are the basics!

743 VISIT SOME GOOD MUSEUMS, GO TO CONCERTS, OR TO THE CINEMA OR THEATRE. I am of the opinion that it is crucial for designers not to be behind the screen all the time, but to move away from that pixel world.

744 RESEARCH. There is no special philosophy about it, I google everything I consider relevant for the project. My daily routine is completed by reading feeds on Google reader and visiting the sites that inspire or educate me such as: smashingmagazine.com, ilovetypography.com, we-make-money-not-art.com, typesites.com.

745 READ BOOKS. I'd recommend Robert Bringhurst: *The Elements of Typographic Style* and a brilliant book by Bill Morggridge: *Designing Interactions*.

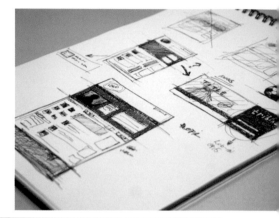

746 WORK WITH YOUR WORKSPACE. I have a really peculiar habit. When starting a new project, before any work is done, I first have to clean the space I am working in, wipe off the dust and clean the desktop in order to start working. As the project is drawing to its end, my work space becomes chaos, in which no one can find their way around, including myself.

747 USE AN ORGANIZER TOOL. At the moment I am using HTC TyTN II for absolutely everything—cell phone, calendar, tasks, e-mails, financial estimates, music, GPS, news... without this device I wouldn't even know when to go to the bathroom!

748 MAKE TIMELINES. Usually we do a timeline of all the projects that we are currently working on at the studio and we allocate our resources according to working days. Such a timeline is constantly placed on our notice board so that everybody knows what everybody else is doing at all times. For every project we make small timelines. At the moment I am trying out an online project management application called Action Method by Behance team.

749 DON'T BE AFRAID TO DO MISTAKES. Love what you do and don't be easily satisfied. Good is the enemy of great. And always iron your designs!

WE TAKE OUR TEA SERIOUSLY

750

ADD SOME ADD-ONS. Firebug, IE Tab, and Window Resizer are obligatory add-ons for Firefox. In everyday life I use a small application called "Tea Timer," made for me by the colleagues. It saves me from leaving the bag inside the cup so that I can be brewing tea for several hours. If you have the same problem, you can download it from our web site!

(R)evolution
www.revolucija.hr

(R)evolution—a drastic and far-reaching change in the way of thinking and idea development. Also a gradual process through which object or subject changes into a new, more complex shape. Located in Zagreb, Croatia, (R)evolution is an all-around creative studio. It was founded in 2003 in a garage by three college friends, Gorjan Agačević, Ozren Crnogorac, and Vladimir Končar, who shared a strong passion for the work they do. Since then, the team has more than doubled in size and it now combines projects from graphic design, complex web applications, web development, interactive multimedia experiences, educational CD ROM's, and multiplayer games. (R)evolution's work has received many awards and it's their goal to constantly challenge themselves to keep developing new and unforgettable visual experiences.

Robert Loeber
www.loeber.co.uk

More than a designer, a picture technician as he defines himself, living and working in London, UK. He enjoys taking a lot of photos, making magazines, designing album covers, creating websites, collaborating with friends, going on road trips, and riding small bikes. Currently working for Urban Outfitters at their headquarters, he is basically a lover of all things creative. Some of his projects include: Poolga iPhone wallpapers, Wood (a themed poster for the eponymous Manchester shop), a poster and animations for Synth Eastwood's *Cycles*, and YCN Live/Whitenoise Gallery *Lets Unite Today*: an A0 digital print on silver paper, defined as an exploration into his limitations of process and color. This last work has been exhibited at Urbn Motion Graphics Studio in Berlin, Germany via the YCN Live project.

751 MOTIVATION. Being highly motivated plays a major role. It's having the drive to always be busy, always have an other project to be getting on with and taking every opportunity that's thrown at you, no matter how busy you are. I'm a firm believer in giving 110 percent in every brief you get involved in. You're only as good as your last piece of work.

752 CONFIDENCE. Be able to talk openly and confidently about your work. This can open up a world of opportunities. Having faith in your own abilities and knowing that you can execute any task creatively and professionally says a lot. Be able to take criticism or advice and learn from it.

753 PERCEPTION/IMAGE. It's not a cynical thing but the way in which you present yourself to the public is very important. This could mean simple things, like sending an e-mail, to the way in which your website looks and works. Pick your moment. Show the right people the right thing at the right time.

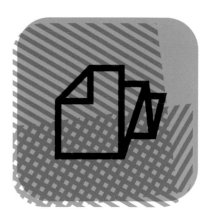

754 THIRST. Have a general thirst for creativity. This doesn't have to necessarily be design but having an interest in finding out new and different things: a piece of technology, a film, or a YouTube clip.

755 ORGANIZATION. Keep everything organized, whether it be by iCal, a diary, or just a well organized filing system. Knowing what you're doing and sticking to deadlines is very important. I learnt this lesson the hard way. I now keep chronologically ordered folders. I've recently started using Stickies. These are a great way to store notes or ideas for a later date.

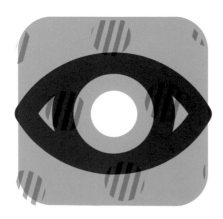

757 INTERNET. The www is the biggest tool for showcasing your work to as many people as possible. Fancy or simple, your website should be a showcase of you. Have fun with it and make something that's easy to update and loads fast (always optimize your images at 60 percent quality for web).

758 COMMUNICATION. Don't be scared to e-mail people telling them about your work. Getting on blogs is a really good way of raising your profile and getting people to remember your name. It's a case of reminding people what you're up to and keeping them informed.

756
KERNING. When using digital typefaces good kerning can transform and drastically improve a piece of work. Or, if done wrong, ruin it. Always watch out for 0 and 1 when they sit next to each other.

759 BACKUP. It's perfectly normal for technology to go wrong over time so always keep regular, external backups. All that important stuff that you couldn't live without should be on an external hard-drive or DVDs and stored somewhere safe.

760 INTEGRITY. Your job should be to create original work. Simple as that.

 timetimetime

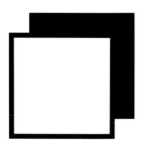

762 Propose yourself for a project only when you are really convinced of what you are doing. Waiting helps experimenting.

763 Search the right media depending on what you have to represent.

764 Dedicate a lot of time to pre-print and interest yourself in inks and tints.

765 Many times something that seems really far from design will take to unpredictable solutions. Don't deny anything.

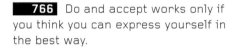 Do and accept works only if you think you can express yourself in the best way.

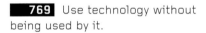 Always sign your works.

768 Lead a regular life. We're not rock stars.

769 Use technology without being used by it.

770 Don't worry about where experimentation can take you, but feel free.

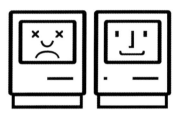

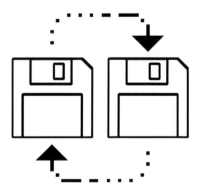

Sabato Urciuoli

www.sabatourciuoli.net

A young visual designer from Turin, he works on concept and its adaptation to visual environment through several media such as publishing, web, photography, and installations. He believes both in the interaction of different media and the one between the user and the message.

His work mainly makes use of typography and the construction/ deconstruction of graphic grids. One of his latest projects is: Play with Sound. Play with Paper. Calendar 2009. It's a 50 x 70 cm poster calendar, intended to map "good" and "bad" days. The idea is to blacken the corresponding square of the day you consider a bad one and leave it blank if you consider it a good one. Musicians can then generate a melody and/or rhythm based on monitored moods of the year, following positive/ negative patterns.

Sacha Leopold

www.sachaleopold.com

A French graphic designer who completed his education at the École Supérieure des Arts Décoratifs de Strasbourg and at the École Supérieure d'Arts Appliqués de Bourgogne. His projects have the objective of exploring and experimenting through a constant questioning of the printing process. His favorite techniques are silkscreen and offset printing, but never in a conventional or banal way. He focuses mainly in print and editorial design—his latest project consisted in curating informative graphic design themed magazines such as *GRATUIT* on the printing world. The aim of the booklet is to enlighten students to a simple approach to printing, defining foundations with illustrated reportages, and printed examples. You can't push the limits if you don't know the basics.

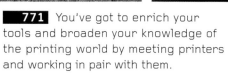

771 You've got to enrich your tools and broaden your knowledge of the printing world by meeting printers and working in pair with them.

772 As graphic designers we have to take the printing process further, especially with self-initiated projects.

773 It's very important to keep having fun! Self-initiated projects will keep you playing!

774 Don't use online portfolios as the only tool to display your work to clients or collaborators. Show a printed version whenever you get the chance.

775
An image is a world-extract. Meeting people that are not graphic designers is very important: farmers, plumbers can be of great inspiration.

776 Be versatile. Learn about web, photography, and video.

777 I don't work with definite timetables, I spend most of my time on the net looking for other projects and on social networks.

778 I try to promote my work in different places with different mediums like art galleries or books. I like to send my work out of France and compare it to different cultures.

779 Don't disown tradition looking for that fashionable graphic design approach, instead analyze the past before everything.

780 Transfer 2D ideas like leaflets, posters, or books to 3D objects and on unorthodox printable surfaces.

781 Conoce la historia del diseño gráfico. A veces, las imágenes de épocas pasadas pueden resultar muy innovadoras.

782 Contempla a fondo la realidad y déjate inspirar por ella. Tienes que tener un cuaderno de bocetos.

783 Build your own image collection while living everyday life or traveling.

784 Remember that the tools are basically the same for every designer. So feed your brain daily with knowledge, culture, and sensibility.

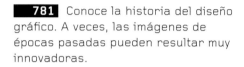

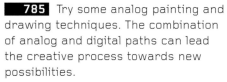

785 Try some analog painting and drawing techniques. The combination of analog and digital paths can lead the creative process towards new possibilities.

786 Take some minutes off the computer several times a day to relax your eyes and restore your ideas.

787 Backup your files automatically.

788 Think of you and your client as a team. Together you can accomplish both his design needs and your need to produce good work.

789 Every job is a potential opportunity to create meaningful visual experiences. Find your playful way to work and have fun.

GEOGRAFIA. LIVRO NÃO-CONSUMÍVEL

EUSTÁQUIO DE SENE
JOÃO CARLOS MOREIRA

GEOGRAFIA
NO DIA A DIA
6.º ANO

editora scipione

790
Read what designers write.

Sara Goldchmit

www.saragold.com.br

During university years, Sara's creative flair developed together with a growing interest for drawing, photography, and typography. After graduating in Architecture from the Universidade de São Paulo, Sara Goldchmit joined the fervent Brazilian graphic design scene. She established and ran Imageria Estudio between 2005-2007; the busy practice created award-winning graphic design projects, mostly revolving around editorial projects for publishing houses and exhibits. She earned her master's degree in design from Universidade de São Paulo and is now a full time lecturer at Istituto Europeo di Design in São Paulo. Since the end of 2008, she spends most of her time traveling, researching, and producing graphic design pieces and illustrations around the world.

Sebastian Onufszak

www.sebastianonufszak.com

Born in Breslau, Poland, Sebastian Onufszak is a visual artist focusing on print, interactive media, and motion graphics. After working as creative director at Parasol Island for more than two years, he is now a self-employed designer and director based in Augsburg, Germany. Since 2002 he has been working for an international range of high-end clients like Rayban, Nike, *The Financial Times*, Blau gallery, SonyEricsson, Mercedes, Red Bull, Jeep. Additionally he is renowned for his experimental live visuals which supported Funkstoerung, Mouse on Mars, Michael Fakesch, and many more. His rich and textured illustration and design works were featured in numerous publications and exhibitions worldwide. He is founder of the artist collective Propagandabuero.

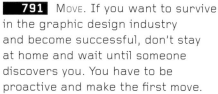

791 MOVE. If you want to survive in the graphic design industry and become successful, don't stay at home and wait until someone discovers you. You have to be proactive and make the first move.

792 OPEN YOUR MIND. Be open-minded about all challenges and opportunities. Try everything. Combining different techniques and experimenting with them is the only way to improve your skills.

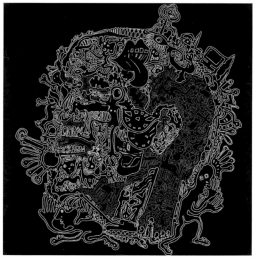

793 GET INSPIRED. Absorb all the amazing impressions of your surroundings. Go outside, be inspired by nature, visit exhibitions, or read magazines and books. Everything can help you gain new perspectives.

794 DON'T COPY ANYONE. Stay self-contained. To get inspired does not mean to adapt other designers or artists. Develop your own personal style.

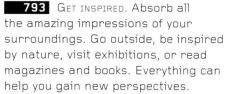

795 GO YOUR OWN WAY. Be committed to the stuff you do. Stand behind your opinion. You don't have to be liked by others, but you should be satisfied with your work.

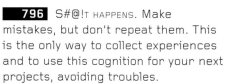

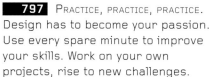

796 S#@!T HAPPENS. Make mistakes, but don't repeat them. This is the only way to collect experiences and to use this cognition for your next projects, avoiding troubles.

797 PRACTICE, PRACTICE, PRACTICE. Design has to become your passion. Use every spare minute to improve your skills. Work on your own projects, rise to new challenges.

798 BE A GOOD TEAM PLAYER. As a graphic designer you mostly collaborate with other professionals. Listen to their arguments to get a broader point of view and to become more critical.

799 HAVE FUN. Above all: enjoy what you do! Who else can claim his profession his hobby? This attitude will facilitate your work and life. And if something goes wrong: It's just a job.

800 BE PATIENT, BUT NOT LAZY. Brainstorming is a creative process, which takes its time. Just like a bonfire you have to feed it with permanent input, until you come to an optimal design solution.

Brief

301 PORTFOLIO. Designing your own portfolio can be one of the hardest projects a designer will work on, as a client to yourself it can be impossible to make choices that would usually come as second nature. I think its best not to approach the portfolio as a project that would then feature in your portfolio, keep it clean and simple and make sure the format doesn't compromise your work. It's important to note that a portfolio should first and foremost show your work, any superfluous design elements included within that should be minimal. I think most agencies agree that the A1 black art portfolios associated with foundation courses are out-dated and unpractical.

802 READING THE BRIEF. Designers often talk about reading the brief; this doesn't just mean forming an understanding to the primary requirements of the client. Most importantly this is about understanding the essence of the clients problem, and thinking of creative solutions that may not be defined in the initial brief as workable outcomes that surpass the result of the original creative requirement. The nature of this thinking has to be relative and reasonable to the client. As an example, it is not to say that if a client has asked for new stationery, a proposal of a new office space that has greater impact on the clients communication with their customer is a valid solution, it is unreasonable and far off the mark from the original scale of the project. It is about pushing the client, but knowing most of all what's fitting for their needs.

803 CLIENTS AND THE "IDEAL CLIENT." In my opinion the notion of the ideal client is misconception, typically it is assumed that the ideal client stands back with little creative input, allowing the designer a free reign with no solid requirements to fulfill, consequently it can be very hard to analyze the outcome of work void of objective and purpose. The reality of the situation is that working with an understanding and cooperative client can produce creative work that addresses real commercial needs in an aesthetic and functional manner. It is the outcome of compromise and understanding from both designer and client that produces the most beautiful functional solutions.

804 SELF-PROMOTION AND CONTACTING STUDIOS. Self-promotion needn't be a soul destroying act of dragging your body to every studio you've ever heard of. Carefully and considerately select a manageable number of studios to target and focus your efforts. Start by making a phone call to find out who is the right person to send a piece of self-promotional work to. Once having sent a sample of your work, call the person you sent it to and ask if they have received it and what they thought, and whether it would be possible to arrange a portfolio review with them. You will soon find that as long as your portfolio is in good shape a few meetings will start to show results and present a range of opportunities. Be sure to stay in contact with these people so they don't forget who you are, you may well be working with them in the future.

10

805
GENERATING IDEAS. When you're starting out as a designer coming up with the right idea can be a formidable task. Along with experience of designing creative solutions and client interaction comes an understanding of what's required and how conceptual qualities are important to the creative process. The most important factor in generating ideas is research, from research comes a knowledge of the subject and creative inspiration in terms of what's possible and feasible within the parameters of the brief. Collating and applying your inspirations into directions can help form the basis of a visual and conceptual approach to the project. It is significant to note that inspiration from a diversity of disciplines is evident in the most original and productive creative solutions.

806 ORGANIZATION. The unexpected reality of being a designer is that the majority of your time is spent doing everything else but designing. With reference material, contacts, and samples filling your studio space it's important that you have a well-organized area in which you can work. Invest in furniture, hardware, and software that will help to organize the digital and physical mass that is so quickly accumulated. It is a great anomaly of being a graphic designer that we are at our most creatively free when we are most organized.

807 PRESENTATION AND VISUALIZING IDEAS. Presenting ideas is one of the most important aspects of a designer's work, especially when you're presenting to a client that may not be used to visualizing without having something in front of them. Ideally a true mock-up will be your most impactive means of presentation, allowing the client to appreciate the tactile aesthetics of the work before committing to go ahead with the production. Although, in most cases this can be an inefficient use of time and can eat into the budget. There are, however, resources to transform your drawings into believable visualizations that can work well in a presentation. Check out www.livesurface.com

808 PURPOSE OF DESIGN. It is noticeable that more and more designers are producing self-initiated projects as evidence of elaborate creative solutions in text and image layout. Aesthetic treatment to design elements, such as typography should hold a semiotic relationship to the context and fit within the conceptual reasoning of the project. It is also important to note that practicing designers will be more impressed with an example of creative expression within the constraints of a working brief rather than in work of self-indulgence.

809 FAVORITE FINISHES. Specifying finishes and materials can be difficult and detrimental to your design if you've had no experience of using them before. A good printer can be very helpful in this respect and provide samples or examples of similar finishing techniques on previous projects. If possible within your schedule, you should request a working proof. Often designers have favorite finishes or materials which have served them well on previous projects, it's important to remember that the specified finishing of a project should always remain appropriate to the design solution and not undermine the legibility or agenda of the work. In my experience simplicity and moderation is the key with finishing, and not to use every trick in the book on one project.

810 VIEW OF DESIGN. *Rational and appropriately designed solutions.* Regardless of the budget and time, my approach to creative work remains consistent. I always endeavor to create solutions that communicate the essence of the idea in a pure aesthetic.

Simon Hughes

www.sebastianonufszak.com

His studio work is primarily brand-orientated, often making use of bespoke typographic solutions to assist creative design and appropriate direction. Hiding cozily in a small-but-well-located studio space, he makes use of the essential resources for good design: books, the Internet, bright natural light, and a kitchen. Working primarily as a freelance designer with his own studio projects, he also enjoys collaborating with specialists to realize design solutions for multimedia and web-based applications.

His most prominent, latest projects include Helvetica, an experimental typeface derived from Helvetica Neue. The typeface is the outcome of an exercise in abstraction and legibility, reducing letterforms to their most basic structural characteristics.

Slang
www.slanginternational.org

Nathanaël Hamon is the graphic designer behind Studio Slang. Born in France, he relocated to the US with his family at the tender age of ten. After earning a BA in Art History, he continued his lifelong interest in visual creation and started working in graphic design. Berlin has been his home since 2000. Why Slang? The linguistic definition shares characteristics with his approach and sensibility— fresh, playful, and constantly reinventing himself. A slang is a vivid and informal language, heartfelt and true to particular groups of people. So far, he's put his signature on lots of posters, record and CD covers, books, typefaces, illustration; mainly dedicated to music, arts, and culture. Examples of his work can also be seen in books, magazines and...on walls.

activate, bring about, ca
start, goad, stir, incita
incitement, bring on, ef
elicit, generate, give ris
effectuate, induce, lead
produce, prompt, prov
ingenerate, make, occas
result in, provocation,
off, touch off, instigat
set in motion, set off, sp

811 DO SOMETHING FOR OTHERS.
What effect does your work have on
society? What are you contributing?
What is your message? Does it make
people think? Does it encourage
discussion? Do you believe in it?

812 USE A THESAURUS. It can help
you find interesting associations and
trigger unexpected ideas.

813 COLLECT. Build up a collection
of texts, quotations, and statements
you find inspiring or that could
become the driving idea for future
projects.

814 EXPLAIN. Be willing to educate
your clients about design. Be aware
that they don't think about design all
day and that it might be quite foreign
to them.

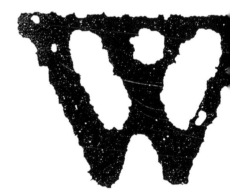

815
Photocopy. Zoom in, zoom out,
lighten, darken. Repeat.

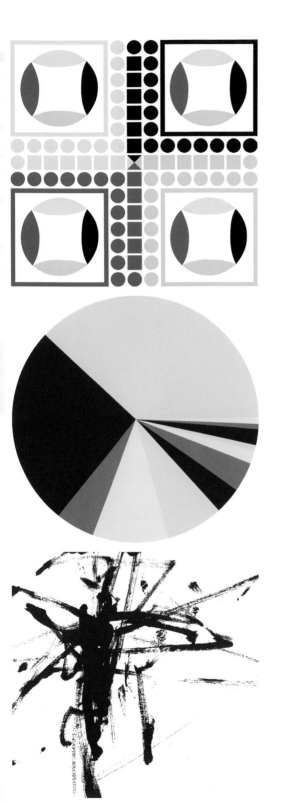

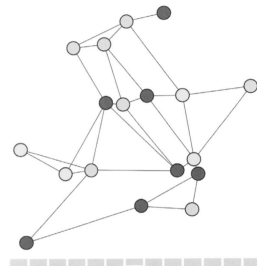

816 It's LIKE A GAME. Define parameters and decide on a few rules by which it is to be played. This helps you be clear about what the focus of each project is and what space you can explore.

817 MIX IT UP. Keep your work fresh by taking on projects for a variety of reasons: creative freedom, exposure, reference, money, portfolio, context, personal interest, volunteer, collaboration, fun, etc.

818 DO IT YOUR WAY. Everybody has a different sensibility, different eyes, different voice, different filter, different edit. Express yourself.

819 COLLABORATE. Two, three, or four heads are usually better than one. Build a network of people to work with.

820 TAKE A BREAK. If you're stuck, put it away, close it, quit it, shut it down.

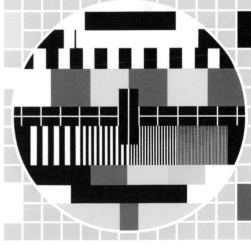

821

WE THINK THAT DESIGN IS MOSTLY UGLY.
A very famous designer told us once
that almost everything he does for
pay looks very bad. Be prepared to
have to make ugly things also.

822   WE THINK THAT NOTHING IS WORSE
THAN THE SILENCE AFTER TELLING AN UNFUNNY
JOKE. A good design concept can be
a tiny source of joy that brightens
the day of your audience. And that
brightens the day of your clients.
To make sure your concepts are
coherent, we suggest describing
yours idea in prose. If an idea isn't
clear in writing, it won't communicate
as a design.

823   WE THINK THAT THE JPEG OF YOUR
LATEST PROJECT LOOKS FANTASTIC ON YOUR
PORTFOLIO WEBSITE. How does it look in
real life? A design's success should
be measured by its actual usage.

824   WE THINK THAT IF YOU WANT TO BE
LUCKY YOU HAVE GOT TO SMILE. A folk song
taught us this.

825   WE THINK THAT DESIGN IS
FUNDAMENTALLY A FASHION INDUSTRY.
Though it is most apparent in
women's clothing, all design work
exists in relation to the tastes of the
time. Having an understanding of
how new tastes develop can help you
figure out how to avoid irrelevancy.
For this we recommend the economist
Thorstein Veblen's *The Theory of the
Leisure Class*.

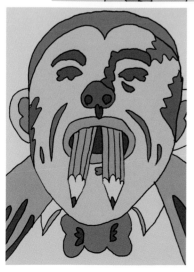

826 WE THINK YOU NEED TO TAKE CARE OF YOUR FRIENDS. We don't think this will necessarily help your career. It may even hurt it a little.

827 WE THINK YOU NEED A HOBBY. At one point design was your hobby, but now it is your job. That is because you are probably a fantastic designer. Now, you need to love doing something that you are terrible at. This will keep you humble.

828 WE THINK YOU NEED TO WORK ON YOUR CREATIVE DEVELOPMENT. Design is your job, but remember when it was your hobby? It was so much fun. An exciting new project without the concessions of clients work will surely take you back to your salad days. Perhaps you should start a self-initiated project or do some pro bono work in exchange for creative freedom?

829 WE THINK THAT YOUR HEART HAS SOMETHING TO SAY TO YOU. When you are finally creating the work you were meant to create, you will feel a warm, encouraging burst of energy. You should try to be happy in the making of things, not with the results.

830 WE THINK THAT YOU MUST BE FREE. You may find yourself down some road that you wish you hadn't ended up on. Don't ever hesitate to change your work, change your style, change your job, change your name, and get yourself free.

Sparrow v. Swallow

www.sparrowvswallow.com

A New York creative studio focused around the work of Philip Fivel Nessen, on his own or with collaborators. Sparrow v. Swallow strives to produce graphic design, web, and illustration projects in a slightly different way than anyone else, focusing on a very personal style and attention to detail. Their extensive list of clients grants them industry creed and they are a well-known name in a New York scene that is—to say the least—saturated with great graphic design studios. They have worked with many editorial, publishing, and institutional clients including *The New York Times*, *Business Week*, *LA Times*, *Playboy*, *McSweeney's Quarterly*, Stefan Beckman, Pearson Publishing, Yale Divinity School, *Illlusive 2*, Die Gestalten Verlag, Threadless Select, and *Bicycling Magazine*.

Studio 't Brandt Weer

www.tbrandtweer.nl

Studio 't Brandt Weer dates back to 1999. A lifetime. Two livelong collections of impressions, images, thoughts, and ideas. And the everlasting readiness to re-enter the school of life. That is the way they work. By having the nerve to wait and the guts to choose.

By brainstorming freely and producing purposefully. By traveling and sitting still. By teaching others and always being willing to learn themselves. It is their own curiosity and eagerness to understand that starts the quest for new visions. Nothing is what it seems. This is

Studio 't Brandt Weer's motto, the formula of their chemistry. In close collaboration with their clients they search for the truth of that specific moment, of that specific challenge. Together with their clients they search for new ways to look at the world and to show it: obvious really.

Ik heb sommigen wel eens horen zeggen: 'ik vind mijn boodschappen belangrijker dan de huur'.

831 Thou shalt have many gods.

832 Thou shalt make thyself many graven images, not necessarily with a likeness to anything.

833 Thou shalt not take the name of thy dreams in vain.

834 Remember the inspiration, to keep it holy.

835 Thou shalt not kill any ideas.

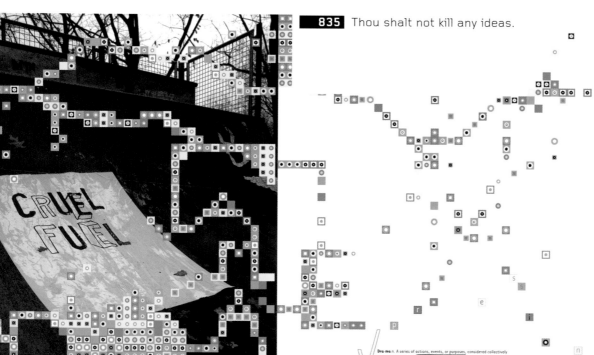

836
Thou shalt play with fire.

Dra·ma n. A series of actions, events, or purposes, considered collectively as possessing dramatic quality.
Ex·pres·sion n. The development or revelation of character and sentiment in art, music, etc., by shadings, nuances, variations in style.

Dra·ma (het; -'s) [1778 Gr.] Toneelspeelkunst.
Ex·pres·sie (de (v.); -s) [1824 Fr. expression]. Gevoelsuitdrukking, gevoelsuiting, uitdrukking van (artistieke) inspiratie naar eigen gonddunken, (ook) expressievak.

"Brengen wil ik haar ook nog wel, als ze vandaag maar ergens gestald wordt."

Bi·ol·o·gy n. The science of life and of the origin, structure, reproduction, growth, and development of living organisms collectively: its two main divisions are botany and zoology.

Bi·o·lo·gie (de (v.), vgl. -logie) [1824 Hoog-Duits, van Grieks *biologos*]. Leer van de levende wezens in de ruimste zin, m.n. van hun levens-gewoonten en -uitingen: *moleculaire biologie, wetenschappelijke* discipline die zich bezighoudt met de chemische basis van erfelijkheid en celdifferentiatie, door de studie van DNA, RNA en eiwitsynthese.

837 Thou shalt commit adultery if needed for creativity.

838 Thou shalt steal anything but originality.

839 Thou shalt not bear false witness against thy principles.

840 Thou shalt not covet that which is thy neighbor's, for thou shalt not need it anyway.

bijvoorbeeld een jonge vrouw met een klein
ij had er echt een potje van gemaakt. was
a afspraken niet nagekomen. had Haag Wonen
aling genomen. Ze had geen euro meer."
s de ontruiming, toen de spullen werden
kt, kreeg Marjolein het even te kwaad.
kleine dochter was er bij. en die bleef haar
oed steeds weer uit de ingepakte dozen
Ik moest toen echt naar buiten, het werd me
veel. Ik heb zelf een klein meisje. Zoiets gun
aand."

der problematisch geval was een
terende 83-jarige vrouw. "Haar dochter
e haar zaken, maar het leek of die het geld
ar moeder opsnoepte. Afspraken werden
gekomen. Ondertussen kon haar moeder
eer zelfstandig wonen.

Het had

na kunnen zijn. Uiteindelijk is ze bij haar
r ingetrokken. Het gaat nu iets beter."

e jaar incassowerk zijn de uitzettingen routine
den voor Marjolein.

Voor mij is

ral een uitdaging: om die mensen weer op
e krijgen. Om sociaal bezig te zijn.

Alles werd afgesloten; water, licht, noem maar op. De bejaarde vrouw begreep het niet, ze was stomverbaasd.

Je hebt mindere dagen, maar ik lig niet wakker van mijn werk. Het is even rot op dat moment, maar het hoort erbij

"...bijna iedereen ver-zwijgt de geldproblemen voor de eigen familie of de buitenwereld."

HUIS UIT

Studio
mit Waar

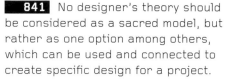

IMAGE NOT FOUND

841 No designer's theory should be considered as a sacred model, but rather as one option among others, which can be used and connected to create specific design for a project.

842 Don't spend your time arguing about which OS is worst. Both PCs and Macs can be fitted out with the same software.

843 For each new project, I try to do something I've never tried doing before. Hence, work is rarely boring.

844 Print design is a wide field. It often goes beyond paper to link up other design activities like product design (packaging), space design (signs), or textile design.

845 Important mottos to have in mind: "Target the logical, then the sensitive," "Form follows the function" (Louis Sullivan). Then there is: "Functionalism (please let me design)" and "Pay your bills."

847 Print design and web design require very different technical skills. They are two different areas.

848 It turns out that killing zombies is a good option when ideas don't come. It won't solve problems, but it's definitely relaxing.

849 I'm used to picking up flyers, leaflets, and brochures anywhere I go. Then, I archive them in boxes. It's another kind of graphic resource.

850 Meeting > analysis of the various contexts of the demand > concept writing > graphic experiments > project > presentation of project to client > (modification of some details) > validation by the client > files completion > manufacturing follow-up > delivery > invoicing > check bank account > buy coffee.

YOU MUST BE OVER 18 TO VIEW THIS IMAGE

846
The number of copies printed for a project is not important. 300 posters or 35,000 brochures require the same attention.

Studio Punkat
www.punkat.com

Hugo Roussel, the man behind Studio Punkat, lives in Nancy, France. He has been working as an independent graphic designer since 2005, after having spent four years in an agency. Specializing in print, he provides answers to problems of identity, editions or signs, for cultural, institutional, or private entities. He also employs his time teaching visual communication in a design school, in workshops, and conferences. He was born in 1976 and can drink about 1.5 liters of coffee per day. Latest projects include: a visual identity for Association de Musique Ancienne de Nancy, the activity report book for Direction des Affaires Culturelles de Nancy, a catalog for the exhibit Victor Prouvé, Les Années de l'École de Nancy, and the magazine *Art Noveaux*.

Subplot
www.subplot.com

Matthew Clark and Roy White are the minds behind Subplot. Matthew took a circuitous route to design. Prepping in high-school for a medical career, he sat on the fence by enrolling in both advanced biology and studio art before fully switching to a fine art major with concentrations in psychology and literature from the University of British Columbia. Roy, instead, was born in London, and graduated from the Mander College of Art and Design at eighteen cutting his teeth early at renowned UK design firms, The Partners and Carol Dempsey and Thirkell. Shortly after he founded his own successful design firm, The Third Man, working with the likes of Virgin Records and the Royal Opera House. Their experiences combined make Subplot one of Vancouver's and Canada's most respected graphic communication practices.

BREWERY/PROCESS

ACTUAL LIQUID

851 START ON PAPER. We believe that ideas should start on paper and only when approved as a concept by the client do we move onto a computer and develop. We are initially asking a client to buy into a concept, an idea, and not a particular typeface, or color, or "look." We find that at the early stages these things can be a distraction for clients and detract from the decision-making at hand, which is: which concept is most appropriate, most relevant and compelling?

852 BEST DESIGN BOOK EVER. *A smile in the Mind* by Beryl McAlhone & David Stuart, published by Phaidon Books. Full of "the" smartest, clever, conceptual design projects from the last 20 years. Second best book ever *Stop Stealing Sheep & Find Out How Type Works* by Erik Spiekermann, for all you type hounds out there, a book that every design student should read to get a grasp that typography is much more than throwing a few typefaces on a page.

853 TIDY FREAKS. Our studio is a 2,000-sq-ft open plan. Both my partner and I are tidy freaks. This is in our personalities but also in an open-plan working environment such as ours it is a must or the place would look like a bombsite.

854 DESIGNERS ARE GENERALLY NOT THE BEST SALESPEOPLE! That's not to say we do not sell ourselves, but we do it through creating great work, ensuring that we then share it with publications and industry magazines and regularly enter into design awards. We find exposure has increased our profile in the industry and has led to generating a lot of new business. Most of our work comes through recommendation.

FULLY LOADED TEA

Created as an alternative to the many watered-down teas and wishy-washy brands, FullyLoadedTea is the bold, opinionated, full-flavoured tea "for a watered-down world".

855 OUR IDEAL CLIENT IS ONE THAT IS A FIT FOR US AND US FOR THEM. It's not a specific project or type of project or project in a certain category. This is something we ask ourselves of any new prospect or potential project. It is based on one simple question and two very simple principles: is this organization entrepreneurial and visionary? If the answer to either is no, then it is likely not a very good fit for either of us. We work best for organizations that are looking to define their category, break the mold of the category norms, stand out, and be different. We look for potential clients who have the ability to recognize good design, and appreciate the value it can bring to their business.

856 ON COMMUNICATION. Like the rest of the world I am completely lost if I leave my matte black pigeon at home.

857 Favorite font: has to be Auto, created by Underware Typehouse in Holland. Amazingly beautiful font with wide range of weights available. The italic has the most beautiful quirks to some of the characters.

858 Font I always wanted to use: Mr. Bear, an alphabet created out of a bear in different positions to create letters. Just waiting for that perfect project to use it!

859 TAKE IT TO THE END. We find that clients come to Subplot for a specific creative product that they see, that is in part to the contribution and what the two partners have to contribute and bring to the table. Any client has one of the two partners as the lead on the project and actively involved at all times.

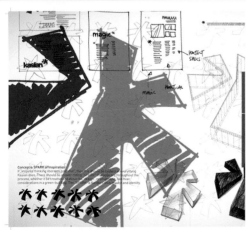

860 RESEARCH IS CRUCIAL. Without it you are designing blind. There needs to be a clear understanding of not only the client and how they currently present themselves, but also the competitive landscape within which they operate. Who are their key competitors? What do they say? What do their brands stand for? How do they present themselves? All these questions are asked. Our job is to help our clients stand out and define their category. Without diligent research one never knows if what you are saying is unique to you or is being said by everyone else in the category too. We will always complete a client audit, a category audit, and a best practices audit, which may not be direct competitors but will often encompass things that the client may not have thought of. Key interviews with corporate stakeholders and even key clients also reveal branding challenges that will be anticipated in our solutions. For larger consumer brands we will work with a research firm to conduct qualitative and quantitative research as is appropriate. This is particularly vital for packaged goods and "revolutionary" branding changes for our clients.

861 To be successful in anything—and graphic design is not an exception—you must have talent, strong motivation, determination, and patience.

862 The best ideas come naturally. All you have to do is sit down, take a piece of paper and a pencil, and get cracking.

863 Learn to enjoy the creative process itself. Don't take the commissions you make or projects you work on just as your job.

864 Try to avoid dull commissions, which don't have any creative air about them. They will do nothing for your creative development. On the other hand, don't be afraid to do interesting projects for free. They can bring you positive experience and good promotion.

865 Always do your job well and on time. If the client is happy with your work he/she is very likely to recommend you to his/her friends, colleagues, business partners, etc.

866 Get good social connections. We received the most interesting commissions through our friends and acquaintances.

867 Think twice before working together with anyone. Even good friends can turn out to be irresponsible when it comes to work.

868 Try to spend less time surfing the web. There is a lot of information, which you don't really need and that will distract you from work.

869 Don't be carried away by trends. Originality is something that attracts people's attention and that is always in demand.

870
If people don't know about you, it means you don't exist. Make the world aware of your presence; create a portfolio on the web and send out news letters about yourself or your studio to the sites and blogs, that are likely to post about you or offer you some work. The more e-mails you send out, the better.

The Sicksystems
www.sicksystems.ru

Starting out as a graffiti crew in 2003 without thinking much about the future, they soon got bored by the limits of graffiti writing and started looking for some new ways of expression. Today The Sicksystems do graphic design, illustrations, identity, typography, and many other things.

In their artwork they look to combine the work of artists, graphic designers, and graffiti writers. They began mostly with commissions for small independent companies founded by young entrepreneurs. Being absolutely free in terms of creativity was a very good experience and helped them grow

as artists and designers. Then more people learned about them, the hype around grew, and bigger commissions started to flow in. To this day their slick street-inspired style has already been chosen by industry giants such as Nike and Miller Brewing Company.

Thomas Williams

www.thomaswilliams.com.au

A Melbourne-based Australian graphic designer, Thomas has worked on a wide range of projects including magazines, publications, web-based design, identity and branding, packaging, super graphics, signage, way-finding systems, and other various print-based design.

He has also worked with a variety of clients including MINI Cooper, Motorola, Ernest Hillier, Southern Comfort, *Lifelounge* magazine, State Government of Victoria, Fairfax Digital, and Melbourne and Olympics Parks. He is contingently working on personal projects as well as running co-owned apparel label Amber&Thomas. His latest project is Twelve Months, Twelve Posters, where a poster using only black and white will be designed representing each month, of the year. At the end of each month, the poster will then become available to purchase online.

871 INSPIRATION. I believe that inspiration is one of the most important parts of the creative process for any designer. I don't just mean trawling through piles of design books and visiting a handful of web pages (although these can be a great way to raise your awareness of the work of other designers), I am more specifically talking about what inspires creativity outside the realm of graphic design. A lot of my work is heavily inspired by my experiences, for example traveling, photography, architecture, music, and general everyday happenings that take place around me. I believe that external sources of inspiration are vital to successful and interesting graphic design.

872 RESEARCH. In my view, research and inspiration are two very different things, and should never be confused. As the old saying goes "knowledge is power" and as a graphic designer this could not be truer. Research is about understanding the client, the brief, and what you hope to achieve. Learn to ask questions and never forget to listen. A good solid base of research is crucial to any design brief, from a logo to a complete visual identity.

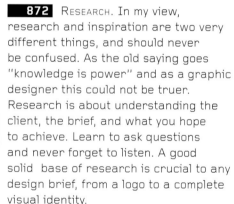

873 BOOKS. Books can be a fantastic tool for any designer and are great for both research and inspiration. A favorite of mine is *Logo* by Michael Evamy. The well thought out selection of logos is printed in limited colors on a beautiful uncoated stock. There are literally thousands of books on logo design, however I can strongly recommend this book for any designer's collection.

874 PROCESS. The processes of design are vast and as varied as the projects themselves. As a designer it is rare to receive two identical briefs, therefore one must approach each project from a fresh perspective. I am a believer that a designer's process should adapt and change accordingly to suit the individual needs of the project (and often client). That said however, each process should be based on a good foundation of research and thorough understanding of the individual project.

875
CRITICAL ANALYSIS. To critically analyze your own work is one of the most difficult things to do as a designer, however it is also one of the most important. The ability to edit your work is a valuable skill you can only obtain through practice. A good editing process will result in a higher quality output and an elevated standard of work. I find when time permits, closing your work and re-opening it the following day can enable you to see things that you may have overlooked previously.

TYPO GRA PHIC POST ERS

876 STYLE VS. SUBSTANCE. With the advancements in computers and software and the amount of graphic design around us, it is more important than ever for design work to have substance. The smoke and mirrors produced by the latest version of Photoshop simply don't cut it. Computers and design software are merely tools for designers, they do not necessarily equate to good design. Good graphic design is produced from a combination of research, understanding, knowledge, and control of the design elements and principals. Some of the most influential design produced today uses only some of the most basic functions of the software currently available. Sometimes stepping away from the computer and picking up a pencil can be the best thing for a design.

877 PASSION. Passion is an essential part of being a good graphic designer and staying passionate about your work is crucial. However the reality is, graphic design is not always glamorous and can sometimes be repetitive and tedious (especially when starting out), so staying passionate can prove to be a challenge. This is why it's important to fuel your passion in other ways. Personal projects can be an excellent way to get creatively inspired, and can be beneficial for you in other ways as well. One of my more recent works, the Twelve calendar, has had more exposure than any single piece of work I have previously done and has proven to be a great way to promote myself and my work.

878 TYPE. Typography is one of the most important elements used in graphic design; it can speak volumes about the designer and the project. I personally only use a small selection and believe that if a designer uses them well, a small range of carefully chosen typefaces is all that's required. As I am merely skimming the tip of this huge topic, the one piece of advice about typography I can give is select your typefaces carefully, understand your selections and how to use them. It is very hard to narrow down to a favorite; however a typeface I have enjoyed using recently is *Apex New* by Thirstype.

879 ENVIRONMENT. This is often the most overlooked part of design, but I feel your environment can have great impact on the quality of your work. There are no specific right or wrongs, as all designers have their own preferences, but a few things I find that work for me are having good light (from my beautiful horse lamp), a comfortable chair, and my book collection at arm's length.

880 ENJOY YOURSELF. I believe above all it is most important for a designer to enjoy themselves and the creative process. Design is not just another job or a career path, it's a passion! I am fortunate enough to be able live my passion every day, and I think if you are willing to make the most of it, life as a graphic designer can be very rewarding.

Apex New Book
ABCDEFGHIJKLMNOPQ
abcdefghijklmnopqrstuv
0123456789&01234567

Apex New Medium
ABCDEFGHIJKLMNOPQ
abcdefghijklmnopqrstu
0123456789&0123456

Apex New Bold
ABCDEFGHIJKLMNOPQ
abcdefghijklmnopqrstu
0123456789&0123456

881 SHAKE AN IDEA. Ideas seem to come easier to me when I'm moving around instead of sitting flat down in front of my desk, hence, I tend to go for a walk at a high pace.

882 STRETCH THE INSPIRATION. I try to get as broad an input of different inspirational sources as possible. It is obvious to go see an exhibition, but from my personal point of view, I get the best ideas when I am far away from design and art. Cycling through the woods, windsurfing on the ocean keeps my mind open and free.

883 POP THROUGH NEW CLIENTS. I get new clients through my website, and sometimes a completed project generates a new project for the same client.

884 THANK A RANDOM COMPUTER PROGRAM. I must say it was a great relief when the Patch Tool was invented. A lot of hours of retouching have been saved.

885 LAUGH THE BRIEF. One can be serious and friendly at the same time, it is just a matter of etiquette. Being able to have a laugh with your client is always a good thing.

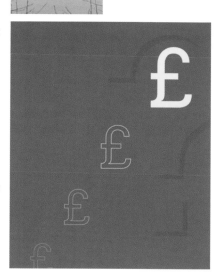

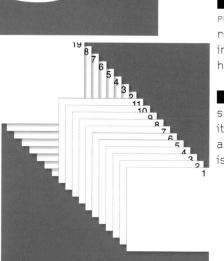

886 ORGANIZE THE COMPLEX. With iCal and the calendar on a mobile phone.

887 PRAISE THE BEAUTIFUL. Mrs. Eaves is a font designed by Zuzana Licko for Emigre in 1996. It is my favorite because of its beautiful ligatures—a very illustrative font.

888 UPDATE THE UPDATABLE. I have a website which I update as soon as I have finished a new project, though it requires a bit of time to photograph printed materials but it is worth it, as the whole world has access to your portfolio constantly. When meeting prospective clients in person, I bring a portfolio containing printed material, as the computer screen never can beat the real thing!

889 PHONE AND E-MAIL. Use telephone and e-mail. Telephone is important to have a direct communication between you and the client, one can tell a lot from the tonality of a voice. E-mail, to list all the things being covered in the phone conversation, you need to have everything written down on paper before starting. Project misunderstandings are never a good starting point.

890 DESPISE THE GLOSSY RINGS. I don't like ring binding, especially not if it is combined with glossy print.

Thorbjørn Ankerstjerne
www.ankerstjerne.co.uk

Originally from Denmark, but now a steady London resident, Thorbjørn Ankerstjerne, graduated in 2007 from Central Saint Martins with a BA in Graphic Design and is currently working as a freelance designer. He enjoys working across a broad range of media from moving image, installations, to conventional graphic design. His latest and most prominent projects include: *FILE*, a magazine focusing on graphic design, art, and visual communication to watch and read. With its accompanying DVD, featuring over two hours of short films, music videos, and interviews, and a commissioned limited print for each issue, *FILE* is a survey of the current visual culture. He also recently curated the Blaak SS09 LookBook, which was nominated by *Wallpaper** as one of the best in 2008.

Tom Crawshaw

www.tomcrawshaw.co.uk

A UK graphic designer working primarily in print with a main focus on identity and branding, Tom is in love with logos, typography, greyboard, books, and the smell of fresh litho print. His approach is to always begin with an idea, even if this can take many forms, be it in the way a design looks aesthetically, what materials are used, or how the production and manufacture is applied. It is often apparent in his work that a simple approach is far more powerful in communicating the core message. Tom tends to strip away anything that is unnecessary, much like a process of distillation and refinement. His latest projects include: invites and wedding stationery for Jane & Dean Watts, a poster for The National Autistic Society, and identity for the band Molly Makes Mistakes.

891 RESEARCH AS MUCH AS POSSIBLE INTO THE SUBJECT YOU ARE DESIGNING FOR. The more information, no matter how general or subject-related, will ultimately give you better scope for developing ideas.

892 IN THE DESIGN PROCESS, THE IDEA DOESN'T ALWAYS HAVE TO BE AN OVERT CONCEPT-DRIVEN SOLUTION. For example, using a relevant or unique material, or perhaps a printing method can form the basis of an idea.

893 IT'S ALWAYS BETTER TO HAVE FUN WHEN BEGINNING THE DESIGN PROCESS. If you're not enjoying it, this will be apparent in the work and the quality will suffer.

894 KEEP UP TO SPEED WITH WHAT IS CURRENT. The wealth of design-based blogs is a great way to get regular bursts of inspiration and also keep you informed of what's new in the design world be it typography, photography, 3D & moving image, web design, packaging, editorial, architecture, illustration, and more.

895 EXPERIMENT WITH PRINTING TECHNIQUES AND FINISHES. It's always more interesting to employ a different process and this can help emphasize a concept or add an extra dimension to the project. Unfortunately, this will almost always have an impact on cost.

896 IT ISN'T ALWAYS BENEFICIAL TO COME UP WITH LOTS OF INITIAL IDEAS ON A PROJECT. If a great idea comes along, present it to the client. If they like it then you may well have saved everyone a lot of time and money. If not, work on some alternatives, taking into account any feedback. This approach doesn't work for every client but can often be a great way to build a good relationship and instill trust.

897 GET OTHER PEOPLE TO LOOK AT YOUR WORK. If you've spent a long time working on something, you often become immersed to the point where you cannot spot mistakes or weaker aspects of a design. Letting others see the work will give you an alternative perspective.

898 WHEN PUTTING TOGETHER A PORTFOLIO, HAVE IT IN AS MANY FORMATS AS POSSIBLE. It is always good to have a printed version to mail out to prospective clients or employees, as well as a PDF version. In addition, having printed portfolio boards are a good way to show many aspects of a project. My personal portfolio for use in meetings is A3-sized but I wouldn't recommend anything bigger.

899 TRY AND SKETCH IDEAS FIRST. Time can sometimes be a problem but if you have it, working through ideas on paper first always helps. Drawing type is another good habit to get into, as it helps you to understand the detail of letterforms.

900 BRAND YOURSELF. It is always good to treat yourself as the client and design a branding package for yourself. It's one of the hardest things to do but if you can't do it for yourself, then any prospective clients or employees will not have great confidence that you can do it for them.

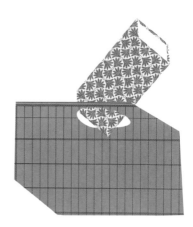

901 For me, being a good writer has been more important than being a good designer.

902 Question all design decisions. Why that pattern? Why that font?

903 To pass on a quote I read from typographer Donald Young: "Don't wait for inspiration, get to work!" (himself quoting Twyla Thorpe).

904 The only way to find out is to do it.

905 Take drawing classes, and draw regularly.

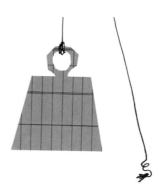

906 Your creative voice will evolve from your natural interests and intuition, but you have to be patient and make lots of stuff you don't like too much along the way. There's no shortcut.

907 As a designer, typography and design history are the two most important subjects you will ever study.

908 Control your inner critic: turn it off when you need to find ideas; turn it on when you start applying your ideas and refining concepts.

909 Experiment with typeface pairings. Lately, my favorite combo is Neutraface by House Industries with Archer, by Hoeffler Frere-Jones. It is recommendable to avoid handwritten style fonts.

910 Surround yourself with creative people. When I was alone in my creative pursuits, someone told me to start having breakfast with similar-minded people as me. This became one of the most important things I did to set me off on my creative journey.

ON

OFF

NEUTRAFACE
archer

Tom Froese

www.tomfroese.com

Tom Froese is a Toronto-born graphic designer, currently living and working in Halifax, Nova Scotia. His work combines design and illustration, which he describes as quirky modern—a blend of mid-century, international, and vernacular styles. For inspiration, he spends time perusing thrift stores for kitsch and old books. Out of all the things he enjoys most about his work, it is the happy accidents that arise when concept, humor, and whatever materials he has on-hand to work with are combined. Tom hopes one day both to teach and to illustrate children's books. Tom's latest projects include: Ourboros General Store Exhibition, a concept store to promote repair and reuse of everyday stuff, and a number of illustrations for the Sustainable City column in *The Coast*, a Halifax weekly newspaper.

Tom Tor

www.tomtor.com

Tom Tor is a design studio and creative collaborative. Whether it be interactive, art, print, motion and/or any other item that inspires the team, there is a profound joy found in applying a unique sense of design and creative thinking. Tom brings ten years of visual arts experience. Having worked with prestigious agencies such as Chiat\Day and Ogilvy & Mather, he cut his art direction teeth on many prominent name brands. Tom believes that creative communications bring together typography, color, and form to fulfill the strategic goals of a company, and deliver creative solutions, and trend-setting design that change the marketing landscape. His view on design has earned him many awards, including the United Nations Award of Excellence in Geneva, International Human Rights Award, and Design of Excellence.

Clean Green   07   GreenDay
Use Environmentally Friendly Products

911 If you can't draw it, shoot it. Use an illustration pen tool to create the vector graphics. Do not use auto trace please.

912 Learn to modify an existing font. Print it out black and white, go over with Pantone markers or a black pen by hand then scan it and put back into Adobe Illustrator, trace with pen tool and go over.

913 Always sketch by hand to create a certain style and look that expresses your individuality.

914 Understand contrasting scale value. Type weights should go from big to small for design and page layouts.

915
When ideas run short, use typography to communicate your visuals.

916 Understand the material you're working with, don't forget to do your research.

917 If you're not working with a good image, learn how to collage your photos into an artwork or convert them in black and white.

918 Understand the use of colors. Please remember less is more.

919 Always ask questions when working on your project. Be ready to have an answer, a good reason, and an idea about your work. It will make things easier for you when dealing with your client.

920 It is absolutely necessary to research all subject matters before you begin working or sketching your ideas.

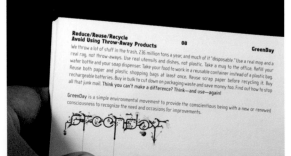

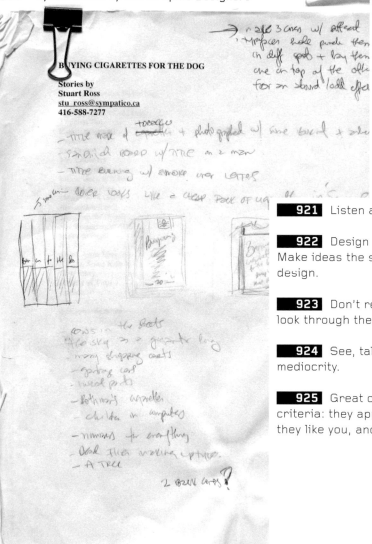

921 Listen and research.

922 Design for the content. Make ideas the starting point of your design.

923 Don't read design books, just look through them.

924 See, talk, listen, read. Fear mediocrity.

925 Great clients meet three criteria: they appreciate good design, they like you, and you like them.

926
Keep pushing your work and yourself to create outside of your comfort zone.

927 Maintain enthusiasm by taking on jobs that excite you.

928 Understand and incorporate strong grids and principles.

929 Know your fonts and how to use them.

930 Embrace the process of production, from beginning to end.

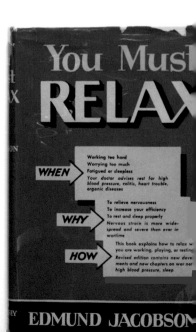

Underline Studio

www.underlinestudio.com

Claire Dawson and Fidel Peña created Underline Studio, a graphic design firm based in Toronto, Canada, back in 2005. The company, relying on its founders' solid passion for graphic design, has since gained international recognition for creating intelligent and engaging design solutions for clients such as Dyson Canada, Harry Rosen, the Young Center for the Performing Arts, the University of Toronto, and Prefix Institute of Contemporary Art. Underline Studio's work has been widely recognized, including gold from the Advertising and Design Club of Canada, *Graphis* and the National Magazine Awards and citations from *Communication Arts*, the New York Art Directors Club, the New York Type Directors Club, *Creative Review*, and the American Institute of Graphic Arts and Applied Arts.

Vertigo Design
www.vertigodesign.it

An acclaimed Rome design agency, Vertigo Design tries to propose a method rather than a style because they consider that all styles are equally functional depending on what they aim to communicate. Consequently the firm tries to attain goals following a rational, logical path and sharply focusing in on the message, thus limiting possible misinterpretations. Vertigo Design works on the many aspects and applications of visual design: corporate identity, corporate publishing, brand image, advertising, multimedia design, and exhibit design. The founders, Mario Fois and Mario Rullo, also teach Graphics and Visual Communications at Università di Roma (department of industrial design) and at the ISIA Roma Design (Higher Institute of Industrial Design).

931 Inspiration can come at anytime—while sitting, eating, driving, or in the office. However, inspiration has to be focused and the important thing is to fully understand what clients want and, above all, their worlds. In this way, developing a visual identity system can truly be customized to last and potentially evolve in the future.

932 A very interesting book which can inspire many ideas at the beginning of a project is *The Art Of Looking Sideways* by Alan Fletcher. Here, a completely un-biased and open-minded approach is employed to explore the complex world of visual communications.

933 Contacting new clients is one of the most difficult and least defined activities. Word of mouth and being passed on by other clients is a frequent method of getting new clients. Once the potential clients have been contacted, a presentation kit of material and, in particular, a (hard copy) portfolio and our website are very useful; normally any choice is based on past projects that clearly show the levels of skill and capacity developed. However, the best way to demonstrate the appropriate expertise successfully is by showing how any visual communication problem can be efficiently resolved despite limited time frames and unpredictability.

934 Professional relationships can be established very differently: they can be reserved with state institutions and large, formal hierarchical companies; or they can be informal with smaller companies where the staff is younger. Perceiving these differences immediately can contribute to avoid an unsuitable presentation.

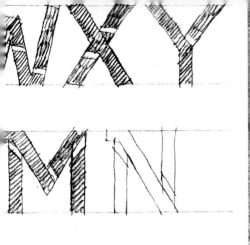

NXY
MN
T

935 For project presentation meetings, slide shows are very useful in showing different stages of idea development—from what the client initially requested to the different solutions proposed.

936 The use of formal grid systems to set out different visual elements (like in layouts) or the use of concept planning to develop a communications system (for instance using coordinating images) can be useful. This approach should however only be adopted once the project is well defined; early on, rigid frameworks can restrict creativity.

937 Vertigo Design has always preferred DIN—an acronym for Deutsches Institut für Normung [German Institute for Standardization], a font we also use for our own logo. Its typesetting origins might have contributed to give it flexibility and that makes it suitable for a coordinated image approach.

938 The most practical and economical solution for project self-promotion is the Internet—both through our own website and other websites specialized in graphic design. However, we have ascertained that with new clients a direct approach with small printed books that set out our case history is the most complete and thorough way of presentation.

939 Our approach is based on "a method, not a style." This means that we can adopt any visual style for potential projects. It is important that each visual feature efficiently contributes to the development of a definitive communications project. With this in mind, we also endeavor to begin developing our projects without any pre-conceptions, listening to our clients and interweaving their proposals and our suggestions into the visually stimulating foundations on which we develop these projects.

940
The type of world we live in implies being overwhelmingly stimulated.
The initial inspiration for any new project can appear in many ways and not always in front of the desk or computer. So now and then it is useful to shut down from the world and end up all alone with a pencil in hand or a laptop. Often jumping from one tool to another seems unintentional but eventually the time comes when all the ideas have to be put in order, in order to select those to be developed further.

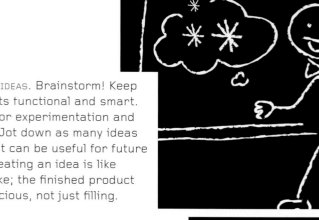

941 ON IDEAS. Brainstorm! Keep your thoughts functional and smart. Leave time for experimentation and production. Jot down as many ideas as you can, it can be useful for future projects. Creating an idea is like making a cake; the finished product must be delicious, not just filling.

942 ON UPDATES. Keep your mind updated as much as you keep your computer. Archive resources such as books, magazines, design tools, left over design conferences material, fonts, photo stocks. This is how you build up a resourceful workspace.

943 ON BEING STUCK. Spending long hours and staring at your screen makes you forget the real objective. Ask for feedback.

944 ON IDEAL CLIENTS. Push the envelope. Ideal clients are the ones who get you carried away with your creativity, and the ones who buy your ideas.

945 ON INSPIRATION. Walk the dog, cook, watch commercials, take a break, it helps you keep your focus on design. Watching commercials is a big source of inspiration; it triggers and stimulates your imagination process. Always make sure to write your ideas. Ask yourself what would you have done if you were the designer...

946 ON PORTFOLIOS. Always keep your portfolio up to date. Customizing your portfolio to clients' needs and expectations is key to success in your presentation, research the clients background on the Internet, market research tools or even by asking targeted questions, a questionnaire would help. I have a printed PDF and website portfolio, it is practical to have all three, especially if you work with long distance clients.

947 Have a favorite font— Gotham.

948 Hate one font—Gill.

949 ON PRODUCTION. You can hate some techniques, but master at least one or two. Great ideas can be transformed into disaster if not well realized.

950 ON HOW FAR YOU CAN GET. A perfect design is pure time management. Leave yourself at least 40 percent of your timeline to improve, tweak, and refine your design. Research different techniques to enhance and add this special touch to your work and client presentation.

Volt Positive

www.voltpositive.com

Ziad Alkadri has a Bachelor in Graphic Design from the American University of Beirut. With over 10 years of experience, his design projects include publications, marketing collateral, print and interactive design. His works have been published and awarded in books and publications such as *Graphis*, *Baseline*, *Eye*, *Applied Arts*, and others. Ziad is creative manager at Xerox, and owner of Volt Positive design house based in Ottawa and Montreal. Volt Positive's multi-disciplinary scope of work includes all aspects of visual communication with a focus on social and cultural design within the small business and the non-profit sector. One of his most acclaimed works is a poster he did in memoriam of the World Trade Center for the New Talent Conservatory.

Xavier Encinas

www.xavierencinas.com

Xavier Encinas is a French Art Director living and working in Vancouver, British Columbia. He specializes in print and typography mainly for art and fashion firms. After graduating in 2003 with a Master's Degree in New Technologies, Xavier started his career in graphic design, crafting websites for small companies, promoting art exhibitions, and creating personal typography projects. In 2005, Xavier was hired by Univers Poche, as head of the Internet department, where he put his marketing knowledge and skill into action. Since 2008, he is the art director and graphic designer for the photography and fashion magazine *Under the Influence*, and, in an effort to promulgate his passion for Swiss graphic design and typography, in 2007 he created the blog Swiss Legacy.

951 Use sketchbook and a digital version to draft the first idea.

952 There are many books you should read! *The Graphic Artist and his Design Problems*, Josef Müller-Brockmann; *Materials, Process, Print: Creative Solutions for Graphic Design*, Daniel Mason and Angharad Lewis; *Grid Systems in Graphic Design*, Josef Müller-Brockmann; *Altitude: Contemporary Swiss Graphic Design*, Nicholas Bourquin, R. Klanten and Christian Mareis; *30 Essential Typefaces for A Lifetime*, Imin Pao and Joshua Berger; *Jazz Blvd*, Niklaus Troxler.

953 Keep your working space clean and minimal.

954 Word of mouth and a personal website will get you new projects.

955 Be informal at meetings!

956 Nothing is as exciting as print projects.

957 Foil is a great finish to add to printed projects.

958 Keep a printed and on-line portfolio.

959 Promotion is important, especially through websites and blogs.

960 Helvetica is still one of the most beautiful fonts.

essing 1.0.1

961 Control the design process from creation to final production.

962 Never show your customers creations you're not completely comfortable with.

963 Do not work alone. Two is better than one.

964 Keep experimenting for your personal enjoyment, fun, pleasure, satisfaction, try to take some time every week to do so.

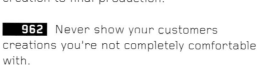

FILE NOT FOUND

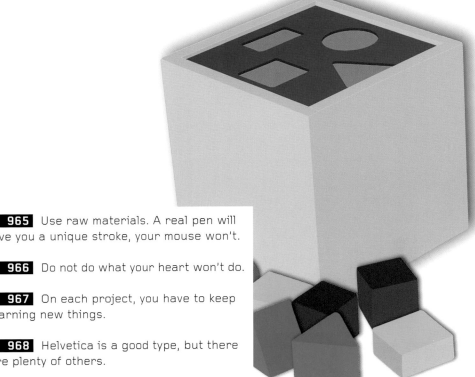

965 Use raw materials. A real pen will give you a unique stroke, your mouse won't.

966 Do not do what your heart won't do.

967 On each project, you have to keep learning new things.

968 Helvetica is a good type, but there are plenty of others.

969 Not all advice can benefit everybody.

970
During the creative process, don't hesitate to use constraints to stimulate your creation.

Young Graphic Designer
www.younggraphicdesigner.be

After his graduation from ERG—École de Recherche Graphique, Julien Bertiaux launched Young Graphic Designer. At first, simply a website to present his works as a freelancer. After two years of evolution learning new ways of expression, Young Graphic Designer has grown and evolved. Yann Braibant, a La Cambre graduate, joined the team in 2008, bringing new lymph and thus making the project a fully bloomed graphic design agency. Their work is characterized by their love of intermingling with all kinds of techniques to research new ways to express ideas and concepts. And their efforts are not unnoticed: their entry for the Folon Poster Contest 2009, a silkscreened A0 on the theme of "I write to you from/about," has been awarded first prize.

Your Friends

www.yourfriends.no

Your Friends is an Oslo-based graphic design studio, founded by Carl Gürgens and Henrik Fjeldberg. Henrik and Carl studied together at Central Saint Martins College of Art and Design in London, and have worked together with various clients ever since. Carl moved back to Oslo after enrolling at Kunsthøgskolen i Oslo, KHiO (Oslo National Academy of the Arts). Henrik graduated with a BA (Hons) Graphic Design degree from Central Saint Martins, and worked this last year at Uniform. They work in different areas of graphic design and develop solutions for identities, posters, music packaging, book design, editorial design, and typefaces. Your Friends work close with other designers, illustrators, programmers and photographers, and with a wide range of clients, both in the cultural and commercial fields.

971 THE PRINTER IS YOUR MASTER. Always challenge your master. Some printers only want to use standard techniques and approaches to the process. If they don't enjoy experimenting, find someone else.

972 YOUR FRIENDS ARE THERE FOR A REASON. Make sure you always have some contacts at hand, and don't be afraid to use them. Showing sketches and explaining concepts to your non-design friends may be surprisingly helpful. Your client is rarely a designer himself.

973 PRODUCTION FOLLOW-UP IS ESSENTIAL. Be critical, use a magnifying glass and make sure the printers understand your requests. Bookbinders are often open for some last minute changes, which might give the project that little extra edge.

974 BE ENTHUSIASTIC. A combination of excellent work, your enthusiasm for the brief, and your eagerness to produce great design always makes people talk, and improves the chances of getting new requests in the future. Enthusiasm also builds friendship.

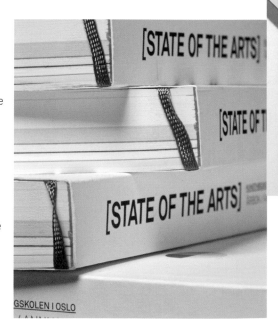

975 NEVER FORGET TO GET READY FOR A PROJECT. Research should always be ongoing. There are always new fields to explore, and several ways to improve your concept and design.

976 YOUR CONCEPT IS KEY. Without a good concept your design may end up as pure decoration. If the concept isn't accepted by your client at first, improve it and make it more visible—do more sketches. When presenting a good concept, the client tends to reach out further in production costs in order to maintain the overall idea.

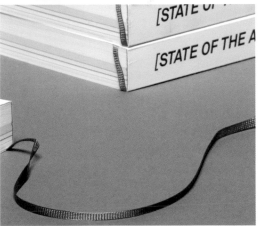

977 THE WHOLE IS MORE THAN THE SUM OF ITS PARTS. All aspects of design are equally as important.

978 TEXTURE. A print design is something that should always have focus on tactility, and it should feel good. Never accept printing on standard paper stocks. Take your time when deciding the desired paper, It should feel right in a rational way. Perfection is always a good thing!

979 DOCUMENT YOURSELF. Good documentation in all aspects of the process may be very helpful. Especially if you're being asked to be featured in a book like this.

980 THERE IS NO SUCH THING AS A BORING BRIEF. Everything has the potential of ending up as a great piece of design, or can also turn out to be the start of new business relations. Try to develop the brief, challenge the clients' wishes, and don't be afraid of getting involved to a greater extent.

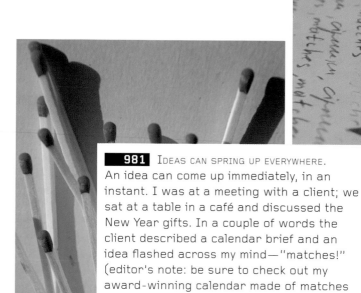

981 IDEAS CAN SPRING UP EVERYWHERE. An idea can come up immediately, in an instant. I was at a meeting with a client; we sat at a table in a café and discussed the New Year gifts. In a couple of words the client described a calendar brief and an idea flashed across my mind—"matches!" (editor's note: be sure to check out my award-winning calendar made of matches on the website).

982 WRITE WHAT YOU HAVE IN MIND. I first describe the idea in words, only afterwards I start designing.

983 MUSIC HELPS. When I work there is almost always music is playing—totally different music. Sometimes it is a particular album over and over again; sometimes it is all the music that I have in my computer.

984 TRY TO KEEP IT ORDERLY. Usually I like it when my work place is in order but it's rare. Whenever I work for an hour, my table resembles a huge dump.

985 GET CLIENTS FROM EVERYWHERE. Some of the clients find you; but it's also good to send business proposals; then there are the regulars.

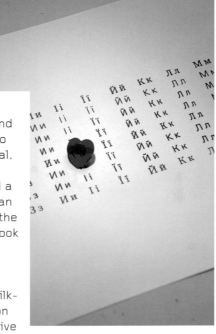

986 WORK ON YOUR LOOKS. I prefer the clothes that make you feel comfortable and confident. Although there are meetings to which you need to wear something special.

987 CHOOSE YOUR FONTS WISELY. I spend a lot of time on choosing a font. As to Roman (English) letters I'm quite satisfied with the majority of them, but most Cyrillic fonts look horrible.

988 VARY YOUR TECHNIQUES. I prefer working with simple graphic forms and silk-screening. Simple forms allow focusing on ideas thus eliminating distracting excessive decoration. Silkscreen printing allows for a hand-made feel for small circulations.

989 PRESENT A PRINTED PORTFOLIO. I often present my portfolio during a personal meeting with a client. Most of my works are worth seeing live, as photos will not tell even half of their stories.

990
WORK ON YOUR ATTITUDE TUWARDS CLIENTS.
I prefer to be open at a meeting with a client. I'm neither serious nor friendly; I try to understand a client and help.

Yurko Gutsulyak

www.gstudio.com.ua

There aren't many designers that can claim to be from western Ukraine near the Carpathian Mountains. Yurko graduated in 2000 as a specialist in the field of marketing and management from the Technological University of Podillia (Khmelnitsky) and worked as a marketing specialist in a sewing factory. In 2001 he started a long-dreamed-of design career after relocating to Kiev. He has worked in an instant printing bureau, in an advertising agency, as a designer in a big corporation, and as a freelancer. Despite having no formal education in art, it's the experience in real life projects that counts. In 2005 he began his own business—Graphic Design Studio by Yurko Gutsulyak. In the course of seven years in the design industry, he's won more than thirty awards in national and international design and advertising competitions.

Zwarte Koffie
www.zwartekoffie.com

Timo Kuilder, or Zwarte Koffie, is a one-man factory creating designs for all sorts of media. A fresh graduate of AKV St. Joost, he is a strong believer in the fact that every design needs a strong idea. He strives to produce uncomplicated, yet surprising designs, hoping that it puts a smile on people's faces. He creates colored worlds where the interactive mix with a strong concept delivery and an intelligent and fresh use of animated characters, colors, and bold typography. His latest project is Living Room. The sound, light, and temperature in the room make a wall come to life. The room will never look the same through a generative visual that shows the state of a living room. To achieve this, the project uses the sound, light, and temperature as input.

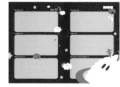

991 Don't constrain yourself using only one tool. A tool can narrow creativity and has limits. Set yourself free and try using other techniques. Or use the current tool in an unconventional way. Graphic design is never a one-time creative eruption, instead it's always a well thought visualization of the idea. Don't let the tool (i.e. Photoshop) lead the design. If you just use the tool to help you realize your idea, you are fine.

992 Make things you think are inspiring. Work on projects that satisfy you and make you happy. Then it will probably make other people happy too. It keeps the quality high and leads towards originality all the time.

993 Be critical about your own work. My portfolio is very compact; I am noticing that this pays off. An average user spends about twenty seconds on my portfolio website. So they probably will only click on a few projects. Make sure these are your best and most prominent on your website.

994 A good logo is simple yet effective. When I design a logo, I usually get stuck at one point. Sometimes it is a good thing to put it away for a while. Other times you just need to keep on designing, and try all sorts of forms until you get the desired result. A trick I use is to abstract the logo/lettering.

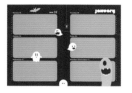
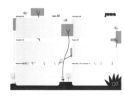
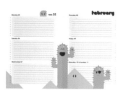
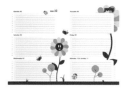
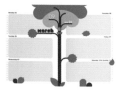
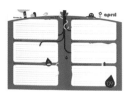

995 DON'T SPECIALIZE. I do illustration, print, websites, and coding. This works for me. I notice that my added value is the fact that I can completely design and build a website myself. So for a basic website the client does not have to hire a developer. This saves them time and money.

996 DARE TO DEMAND A GOOD BRIEFING. If something is not clear just ask or call your client again. Boundaries set by a briefing also help me to create an idea. I cannot create something if there are no limits.

997 DO NOT REPEAT YOURSELF. Try to renew yourself in every piece you make. I think it's rather hard. Because of time pressure I tend to do something that worked well before. But I strive to experiment and treat every single project like it is my first and last.

998 WORKING IN A SMALL TEAM HAS MANY ADVANTAGES. Together with Jankees van Woezik, a talented developer, we created the website for Blond Amsterdam. Because we had the opportunity to work on the project at the same time, we were very flexible. Small changes could be done fast. When the developing gets done afterwards, the end product doesn't always look like it is designed. Working on the project in the same space and at the same time, improves the workflow.

999 GET INSPIRED BY EVERYTHING. Take pictures, look around you. I always visit media bookmarking sites like ffffound.com, dropular.net, and ilovenewwork.com to see fresh work. The possibilities are endless.

1,000
YES, DESIGN CAN MAKE YOU HAPPY. It's an inspirational talk by Stefan Sagmeister on TED (www.ted.com). Here he talks about moments in his life that made him happy and notes how many of these moments have to do with good design. *Things I have Learned in My Life So Far* is another of his inspiring publications. A good quote is "Having guts always works out for me," referring to smart design. I agree, because I think holding back kills improvement.

GOOD DESIGN

LOOK AROUND YOU DESIGN IS IN EVERYTH

THIMM'S SELF-TAUGHT LANGUAGE SERIES
ITALIAN SELF-TAUGHT
A NEW SYSTEM
FOUNDED ON THE MOST SIMPLE PRINCIPLES

PRACTICE SUSTAINABILITY
OR THE BABY SEAL GETS IT

DON'T FOLLOW